GW01046302

THEY HANG ME
IN TOKYO

BANKROFT BOOKS

Contact information for Bankroft Books– info@bankroftbooks.com

ISBN: 979-8-9894317-0-0 (paperback)
ISBN: 979-8-9894317-1-7 (ebook)
ISBN: 979-8-9894317-2-4 (hardcover)
ISBN: 979-8-9894317-3-1 (audiobook)

Ordering Information:
Special discounts are available on quantity purchases by corporations, associations, and others. For details, contact info@bankroftbooks.com.

THEY HANG ME IN TOKYO

*A Barbarian Artist's Life-Changing Journey
to Master Nihonga, the Traditional Art of Japan*

ALLAN WEST

To the people who know what they like.

I can paint for them because of the craftsmen who make it possible.

Arigato.

CONTENTS

MY QUEST

I *looked down. My fingers were covered in blood.* I glanced around the half-empty subway car, hoping nobody had noticed. I pulled out some pocket tissues and tried to wipe off all the telltale signs before I arrived at my stop. How much was on my face?

I was so anxious about the upcoming encounter that I hadn't been able to sleep the night before. Breakfast that morning had also been impossible, and I had spent all afternoon on the train.

I pinched my nose and raised my head, looking up at the map above the door. The next stop would be it. I jumped out at the station and, looking around frantically, found a restroom.

The mirror showed that I had been lucky to stop this nosebleed in time.

I gave my ticket to the man at the gate and went up the stairs. The sun hit me full in the face. My head throbbed in the heat and glare. No, I wasn't going to let this keep me away.

"What next?" I said to myself as I thought of all the things in the last four years that had kept me from finding this place. The anticipation had been too intense—and now this excitement.

I needed to make a good first impression.

You would think that something as simple as looking for a store would be easy. But it took four years of failed attempts searching in Japan to finally find it.

This journey had required me to learn the language, and even then, it turned out that most Japanese people didn't know anything about what I was looking for. The world of traditional *nihonga* painting was foreign even to most of the Japanese people I met, so they had no idea what these special permanent pigments made from gemstones were or why I would be so obsessed with them.

Years ago, I had a hint of their existence from a casual comment. From there, my quest began. That was in the early '80s, and the most powerful search engine in the world, the Library of Congress, came up with nothing.

So finally, in 1985, after having saved up for months, I was determined to buy some of these legendary fine pigments. I could, at last, go home and live my long-held dream of painting with them all day long and into the night.

To find this place in Tokyo, I took the day off from my job at the Tsukuba Expo. But after arriving at the station, I got lost. It didn't matter. I was so very close. I only hoped I could get there with enough time to drink it all in before closing time.

My friend Sach had found me an old edition of *Bijutsu Techo* magazine. In it was a special section on nihonga. It mentioned this shop and how to get there, and its pages were tattered from time spent in my pockets.

As I approached the storefront, I caught sight of a wooden signboard in the window. The board had seven circles carved out, each filled with a different color. This traditional signboard of the pigment seller didn't match the functional concrete building it was in. I tried to slip in unnoticed, but the bell rang out as I closed the heavy glass door behind me. A distinguished-looking customer stood at the back of the shop.

Full-length shelves filled with glass jars of pigment lined the walls. Each color was arrayed from its darkest iteration to almost white. There were thousands of jars that fronted the shelves, with another row behind. In the center were cases containing brushes, and on closer inspection, I also saw some expensive antique inkstones and water droppers.

The price label on one of the colors was 4,600 yen per *ryo*.

I didn't know what a ryo was, but I did know that if I used this green in my forest paintings, the trees would come alive.

I found a jar with a brilliant, glowing blue. I took the jar from its shelf, pulled off the stopper, and peeked inside.

No chemical color could have such hypnotic beauty. Everywhere I looked, the pigments were made from natural minerals—ground gemstones—lapis, malachite, agate, and jasper.

Another jar was 5,000 yen per ryo. I again wondered how much pigment was in a ryo.

I imagined a painting with such tantalizing color in the background would emit a low, musical hum. I would never again be satisfied with the plastic superficiality of the chemical pigments I had been using.

In the back of the store, I watched the man behind the counter. He was a fidgety gentleman with a bald pate and a plain gray cardigan hanging on his shoulders.

He placed a sheet of waxed paper on a small scale, then ceremoniously removed the stopper from a jar. Rolling it, he scooped out small spoonfuls of brown powder, tapped the weights, and then flicked a small corner of the spoonful back into the jar.

Tap, tap. The pile of color wouldn't amount to more than two bottle caps' worth of powder. He deftly picked up two corners of the paper, tipped the pigment into a small sachet for the customer, and gave it a snap so the last few precious grains would fall in place. There was something almost poetic about this transaction, and I eagerly anticipated my turn.

After exchanging pleasantries, the customer was gone.

It must be my turn. I wasn't sure of the best approach. Should I take the jar to the counter? How much should I request?

The man came out from behind the counter. His eyes flashed. "Put that back!"

I froze, perplexed.

He sprang forward, took the jar from my hands, and replaced it on the shelf with exaggerated care.

"No! We do not sell to hobbyists," he hissed.

My hand went to my wallet so he would know I was willing to pay. But I could see it wasn't about the money.

He folded his arms over his gray cardigan, and I knew it could only get worse. Breathing heavily through his nostrils, he pointed to the door.

"This store is only for the patronage of the great master painters—those decorated by the emperor."

I got out. It wasn't quite closing time, but he locked the door behind me.

My knees felt weak as I walked down the hill. My heart was pounding, and I needed to sit down.

Turning the corner, I saw a café. I sat on a tall stool, opened a menu, and faced away from the kitchen. I did everything I could to suppress the anger and frustration that came from this fruitless journey. I'd spent five years in search of this place, for what?

A voice caught my attention. "What would you like to order?"

All my efforts had come to nothing. My voice quavered as I ordered.

After years of searching, I had finally found the kind of paint I needed—but I could not have it.

What was I supposed to do?

I pulled out my pocket dictionary and flipped the pages. Even the words used in the nihonga world appeared to be different from ordinary Japanese. It didn't have any context where ryo was explained as a unit of measure.

I had taken the job at the Tsukuba Expo expressly so I could find this pigment store. Well, I'd found it—and now I had to return to a job I hated without the hope that once motivated me. The thought made my face hot and my eyes burn.

When the food came, I struggled to swallow.

I sat at the table, trying to understand what had happened. In my ignorance, I had presumed to enter a sanctuary where only a select few were welcome—a *Japanese* few. It felt like a permanent rejection. Had the shopkeeper found my breaking point? No. Quitting was not an option. I could not forget those colors. But would I ever see them again?

I opened the magazine in my hand to read about the decorated masters. Perhaps their pupils had access. It would take more years of searching for a mentor. And who knew if any of them would even accept me?

Would I ever be able to overcome my innate foreignness? I felt like a barbarian.

I'd clumsily pushed my way into where I was unwelcome. The typical Japanese person would've picked up on such cues. I hadn't. I just hadn't known any better. Like a barbarian, I had been unintentionally destructive, and it wasn't the first time.

The sky was darkening outside, and the expo dormitory was four hours away. Deeply disappointed, it was time for me to drag my tired body home.

I longed to be where I didn't feel so foreign.

As the train jostled me away from that day's events, it jogged into my mind a memory of seven years before when I'd felt even more of a barbarian, and yet almost enthusiastically welcomed.

THE BARBARIAN EARNS
A MERIT BADGE

It was as a 16-year-old Boy Scout living near Washington, DC, that I first learned about this barbarian in me.

In a remote area of the woods, I sat for three hours, recording my observations for the nature merit badge. I was to identify the plants and animals I saw.

When I first sat down, I listed the plants I could identify. I noticed my breathing caused the leaves to rustle. If I expected to see any animals, I mustn't move or make a sound. I tried to make each breath quiet and shallow.

At first, all I could hear was the blood pounding loudly in my ears. Then I heard the feet of a beetle tapping against a dry leaf. After 40 minutes, ants, millipedes, and pill bugs ventured out in businesslike fashion. A fly. An earwig. Soon, larger insects arrived, clicking and jumping across my field of vision.

In time, by remaining quiet, waiting, and listening, a few of the forest's smallest inhabitants revealed themselves and came to explore inside my shirtsleeves and pants legs.

How long had it taken this inchworm to make it to my forearm without my noticing? It stopped and raised itself on its back pairs of legs, the upper body waving as if trying to make me out. It felt like a gesture of friendship.

It took the animals time to sense I had come in peace. The sound of the pencil on my notebook was loud, so I wasn't able to record even a fraction of what I heard or saw.

Birds appeared, whirring, thrumming, and tapping. A woodpecker's hollow percussion echoed from all directions. I didn't dare move my head. Sound and motion, flittings and dartings, surrounded me. Having blended into the woods, I experienced a streaming cacophony from the forest.

A chipmunk and a raccoon arrived. A deer's intrusion briefly silenced the area until a bird call seemed to signal all was clear.

The air began to cool, and the color of the forest deepened. Even this subtle change filled me with awe. My understanding had broadened, and the thought of returning to a narrow human awareness hurt. I was not ready to end this day of enchantment. But I knew that people would come for me if I didn't return.

As I arranged my legs to stand up, all went still. I hesitated. What had been a confusion of life and motion disappeared, replaced by silence. I'd entered a world normally inaccessible to huge lumbering humans, unaware I was mashing anthills and collapsing mole tunnels. How insensitive I'd been!

By getting up to leave, I became a monster, feeling larger and more destructive than before. As I followed the trail back to my tent, it seemed wrong to tread there, knowing of all the life underfoot.

I'd need to catch up on documenting all I'd seen.

Most Boy Scouts tried to avoid working on the nature merit badge. It sounded boring to them. But of the 24 merit badges I earned, that's the one I remember best. We all bring our own past to whatever art we create. And in my thoughts, I often revisit that forest.

Even at that age, I especially admired artists who were inspired by the beauty of nature. I wanted to be that kind of artist too.

Looking at art—and making it—was my joy. It took me a long time to understand it was considered uncool. But by the time I understood that, I was already completely hooked.

I was at that age when I made this realization, and besides, I had the comfortable sanctuary that was my art. Most of the kids my age were interested in cars and sports. But by then, my understanding of both those things was completely inadequate. People around me had already settled into that cool territory. The culture and language of sports were closed to me.

I loved getting my hands dirty in the creation of art. I was also exhausting the local libraries, reading books on art and artists. I soon moved on to the Library of Congress and relished the ranks of card catalogs with which I could look up anything.

Most weekdays were spent taking adult education art classes after school. Weekends were filled with the Smithsonian's galleries. The artwork there became like familiar friends.

I lived for art.

FREEDOM OF EXPRESSION

I *remember around that time seeing an artist being* interviewed.

He said, "I would die if I couldn't paint."

That seemed like an exaggeration to me then. It would be much later that I would remember these words and recognize those feelings. For me, the challenge of painting was more engaging than anything and the most fascinating thing to do.

I thought about the consistency of paint when I brushed my teeth, and while I waited for the school bus. I thought about mixing colors during Mrs. Kemp's math class and when I should have been doing my homework. I thought about the choice of brushes while I ate dinner, and I dreamed up my next painting in my sleep. It was like a puzzle. I worked on one part of a painting, and it caused a cascading effect as each other element of the painting would need to be adjusted accordingly. But if I was lucky, I ended up with something I liked to hang in my room.

My mother took a class in portrait painting before I was a teenager, and I fixated on that. I thought that was an almost-superhuman thing to do. Out of a few materials, a whole person could be expressed. I realize now that during that few months' time, she painted just a handful of paintings. They were of anonymous people who posed for her class. But it made a big impression on me. She freely shared with me what she learned, and I consider her my first art teacher. I realized it wasn't just the technique and materials I liked. I could see that if I got good enough, I might be able to express complicated emotions or ideas. One day I might even create worlds I'd like to inhabit.

For a while, I also painted portraits, but I soon learned that as fashions and hairstyles change, and as people age, portraits become problematic. I took to focusing on capturing the essence of a person rather than only their looks.

When I recently mentioned to my mother how I was interested in watching her paint, she sounded surprised. Painting was not so much a part of her identity as I had thought.

My father was an analytical thinker who studied philosophy, then became a lawyer. He saw my mother's painting as a pleasant pastime for her, but couldn't see how I, with a future full of possibilities ahead of me, would want to seriously pursue the path of a starving artist.

I saw my parents' marriage as one of two people from quite different cultures. I saw it as the happy union of a bright, creative mother and a prudent, intellectual father.

While I was impressed by my mother's portrait paintings, I became obsessed with painting the beauty of plant life. This began one day when I was in elementary school. We were forbidden from entering the woods. But I gave in to temptation and wandered into the woods behind the school to explore the clearing. The timing was perfect. The scene was filled with wild blooming wisteria. I felt as though I had been the only person lucky enough to have been welcomed there.

Vines chased through the space between rigid tree trunks. There was a subtle fragrance, light filtered through the vines and leaves, and the hanging blossoms moved with the air.

This unexpected experience felt almost unendurably perfect. My work now may draw from a variety of sources, but I want it to have a similar effect on the viewer as I felt on that day.

I enjoyed other creative pursuits and dabbled in ceramics, making pots and bowls. Starting at 14, I was commissioned to paint stage backdrops for a drama troupe. The functional things I made were noticed and acknowledged.

But more than thing making, I could see myself spinning whole worlds in paintings. They'd be the physical incarnation of an emotion or a philosophy.

I didn't understand how my paintings could be beyond my brilliant father's grasp. He seldom made comments about my work. On the two times I was brave enough to outright ask for an opinion on a realistic landscape, he said that he "didn't get it."

Maybe I would just have to paint better.

As a lawyer, Dad prepared thoroughly for court cases. I often saw him in the car rehearsing speeches to himself as he drove. His desk was piled with reams of papers and books that he heavily underlined and annotated as he read.

Similarly, I tend to write marginalia as I read, and I suspect I also got my enjoyment of public speaking from him. For my dad, words were tools, and their precise choice was necessary for his profession. I found his sort of rigidity the opposite of what's required of an artist. It takes different tools to create something of beauty that's thought provoking and also compelling. I believe great art needs to be a balanced appeal—not only to the mind but also to the heart and the eye.

Like his father before him, Dad placed importance on his appearance and dressed carefully—mindful of the impression he made in court.

In my teens, he wanted me to be more aware of how I looked, and he checked my appearance before I went out. After returning, I experienced routine debriefings with my parents while sitting at the foot of their bed.

Above all, I remember my father asking not only who was there but also what they were wearing. It made me feel as if I were a project—an accessory. I knew he was hoping my appearance was suitable according to what others were wearing. With my mother, I was mostly concerned that I got the paint out of my clothing.

An elderly couple, the Telfords, sometimes visited. They were always kind enough to look at my drawings approvingly.

The Telfords had been in the same social circles as our family for three generations. Dr. Telford, a professor of anatomy at George Washington University, was a kindly gentleman with white hair, light-blue eyes, and a distinguished demeanor. His wife had a warm heart and formal bearing. Her hair, like soft spun glass, was always perfectly coiffed. They took their influential relationship with us children seriously.

Some people have godparents. Our family had the Telfords. They provided me with a valuable perspective from outside the family. They're the only people I can remember who didn't try to encourage me to aim for a different career. On their visits, they would always ask me more about the creative projects I brought from my room to show them.

My parents and other relatives suggested engineering or architecture might be better. They didn't get it. There was no way I was going to take their advice to abandon painting flowers and trees. A career in art was what I wanted, but I knew it would be difficult to attain. Biographies of artists made that clear.

I knew if I wanted to make an art career happen, I'd need a plan.

4

MAGPIE IN A
SWALLOWTAIL COAT

My third-grade teacher, Mrs. Baer, said if we decided early enough what we wanted to do in life—and if we planned step-by-step to reach that goal—by golly, we could make it happen! That's when I got serious about taking art classes.

At nine years old, I signed up to take my first real oil painting class. There was some confusion when I appeared in the classroom. They checked my name against the one on their list. They apologized for not explaining it was an adult class when I registered. I could participate if I didn't mind their instruction being directed toward the rest of the students. I was too excited about the instruction to think how I must have come across in an oversized shirt smelling of my dad's cologne in a circle of serious painters. But I was serious too.

And I'm grateful for the art teachers and classmates who assimilated me and my enthusiasm.

I loved my classes at Glen Echo, a repurposed Chautauqua village, and later at the Corcoran Museum's art school. When I wasn't creating art, I was reading about it.

I wasn't just motivated to take art classes; I also wanted to know more about what it was that made great art great.

At the Smithsonian Institution, I saw Jackson Pollock's *Number 3*. The caption said it was painted with oil, metallic enamel, and cigarette fragment on canvas. The skeins of swirling color seemed to flit and dart, enveloping me as I approached. It reminded me somehow of my experience in the wisteria forest.

It took me some time to find the cigarette fragment trapped in the net of paint. That cigarette may have been an accidental flaw, but it in no way diminished the painting. If anything, the contrast accentuated the painting's perfection.

It was the 1970s, and my classmates went to great lengths to express their individuality. That usually played out in punk rock fashions or not-so-subtle references to drug culture.

Those things scared me and were so beyond my experience that, in such gear, I would have been an obvious fake. There was also a classmate's father who ran a clothing store that marketed to us at various school events. Wasn't that how adults exploited our teenage rebellion? Fashions, music, and entertainment were all subtly marketed to us. Were we actually rebelling, or were we falling in line?

I usually wore what was there. It was the button-down oxford shirts, corduroys, and loafers I received as Christmas and birthday presents. This is how I was encouraged to wear the kind of outfit my father approved of. But I might rebel by wearing the outfit I bought with my lawn-mowing money.

Most of my money went to art supplies, but I loved to visit junk shops, antique fairs, and stores that sold old things. It was like a window into a different time and place. Most of the things I bought that way were well made. Not only were they made to last, but they were usually cheaper than buying new items.

I found a Victorian woolsack morning coat, boiled shirt, and high-buttoned waistcoat. To complete the outfit, I bought a cummerbund, a celluloid collar, and wing tip shoes. My button-up spats came with a button hook. This look was my rebellion against the system that I felt was gradually trivializing discipline. This starchy formality was what happened when I celebrated my inability to fit in and took it to the next level. I guess I took things a little too seriously. But I also looked good in those clothes.

The yearbook had a photo of me captioned "Allan West in his usual getup." Though I didn't expect acceptance, I appreciated this acknowledgment and took the gentle ribbing as affirmation. I saw this as the most genuine expression of myself. In retrospect, this feeling takes on an added significance. I see now how I was a bewildered youth unable to adapt to his times. It has taken time to understand that about myself and how I need to minimize the stresses this creates.

I felt the same way about music.

Though I could hear a great variety of popular music on the radio, I couldn't keep up. But my grandfather's phenomenal collection of classical music was always available, and it spoke to me in a more lasting way. The music had me seeing colors and feeling emotions.

The beginnings of paintings often started with what I saw when I heard music.

I learned to appreciate art—whether musical or visual—that was well made and could endure the ages.

Fortunately, I was able to attend an art-focused high school. My teacher, Walt Bartman, was an inspirational teacher and an incredibly gifted motivator. He called a group of us his magpies and guided us on a sketching tour through Europe.

I sent artwork to various juried competitions. A print was selected for exhibition in the National Collection of Fine Arts, and when a painting of mine won a county art award, Mr. Jerome Marco, the school principal, asked if he could display it in his office. This gave me the courage to request a second hour of art at the end of every day.

He allowed me that extra hour in place of a language credit so I could participate in a special program. I was probably breaking a few rules, but with the principal's understanding. Twice a week I left school an hour early so I could volunteer at the Smithsonian.

I worked at the National Collection of Fine Arts, as it was then called,[1] and in the silk screen studio of the Renwick Gallery, preparing screens for hand-printing posters.

I also worked in the immense slide library where photographic slides on file documented every work of art in all the Smithsonian's collections. I was responsible for locating the slides and sending them to curators who needed them for exhibitions or for books they were writing.

There was a slide for everything that had been owned by affiliated

---

1   The museum I knew as the National Collection of Fine Arts was housed in the old Patent Office Building. It is now called the Smithsonian American Art Museum.

museums or borrowed over the years. Thus, I became well acquaint-ed with many artists. This helped me immensely in my knowledge of art history.

5

MY LITTLE GREEN FRIENDS

I *had a lot of friends. I usually met* them behind supermarkets or drug stores. At first, they were rough around the edges and looked a little seedy. Most were limp, but what would you expect? They had been turned out and were trying to survive on their own.

I took them out of the heat and gave them a drink of water and a place of honor by my bedroom window. It wasn't always easy to find out their names. It took a few trips to the library to identify them. I usually gave them a bigger pot and surrounded their roots with rich, nutritious soil.

I found the still-supple trunk of a tree fern that had lost all its fronds and nursed it back to health. In time, it created a canopy of fronds over my bed. I also rescued what I later learned was a coffee tree. The light from my window filtered through its branches.

Looming over my bookshelf was a monstera. It created an awning under which it was fun to read. Grape ivy, Creeping Charlie, and ferns covered my desk and chest of drawers.

I liked to imagine they shared my taste for classical music. I found that cases of flinty 78 rpm records were practically free at junk shops. To highlight the plants, I painted the walls of my bedroom red.

I let my parakeet Bobby fly freely in my room, which my father called the jungle. In ceramics class, I made a fountain and connected it with an aquarium pump to circulate the water. It contributed the sound of water as well as amusement for the bird.

Bobby woke me up every morning. After greeting me enthusiastically every afternoon, he sat on my shoulder and watched me draw or study. Sometimes he would whisper to me or weave through my hair. If he felt especially affectionate, he would feed my ear with seeds.

Lying in a hammock under a canopy of trees, I plotted out my future and decided I wanted to seek out and disseminate beauty through art. What could bring more joy than the beauty of nature?

I loved painting plants, but the stiff, viscous properties of oil paints made detailed work challenging. Besides, turpentine or thinners, materials you must use when painting with oils, gave me a headache, so I was already less than enthusiastic about using oil paints. But oil paints were just about the only way to paint something permanent.

The backdrops I painted each month for a drama troupe of amateur actors while I was in junior high and high school only had to last the month of the performance. This was my first experience as a professional, creating art to fill a need. The sheets, stretched onto wooden frames, often got holes punched in them during scene changes. Eventually, the sheets needed sewing too.

The liquid house paint I used was free and easy to work with, but it would eventually flake or fade. At least I could use lines to outline or create detail. This became frustratingly absurd when I tried to make art. When using viscous oil paints scaled down to the size of a picture, the highly textured canvas and thick paint made painting fine lines impossible. Thinning it made it liquid but, unfortunately, also translucent. There had to be a better way.

MY WORLD-CHANGING
INVENTION!

I *decided to invent a better paint myself.* Perhaps I could come up with a formula that was both opaque and liquid. I learned that paint itself required pigment, something that provided the color. But it also needed something to bind each of the grains of pigment together as well as onto the surface I was painting.

Watercolors and dyes fade, so I wasn't going to work with them. If I spent the time working on something important enough to express, it would have to be permanent.

Perhaps the edgy, punchy paintings that currently grabbed the art world's attention would not always be important. And people may or may not have liked the flowers and trees I was painting. But still, only those that survived the ravages of time would remain to be appreciated or rejected in the future.

I went to the Library of Congress to study painting techniques and learned that the Renaissance artists didn't use cotton canvas. They used linen with a tighter weave, which I found a less distracting material on which to paint.

More research into the history of painting techniques taught me that the kind of gesso undercoating we use now hadn't existed then either. They used something called rabbit-skin glue—a smelly,[2] translucent liquid that was made by boiling the protein out of rabbits.

Luckily, I didn't have to extract it from rabbits myself. I could get rabbit-skin glue at the art supply store. I learned that framers use it now for gold leafing frames.

Rabbit-skin glue soaks into the linen and creates a barrier against the oil, preventing it from seeping into the fibers and rotting or going rancid.[3] To melt it without scalding, I had to heat it in a double boiler.

With the protein, it was possible to sand and repaint to make the surface smooth.

Next, Renaissance artists used marble dust mixed with linseed oil to create a glassy white base coat. I could tell this was going to be much better than anything I had bought and used before. Unfortunately, this white base took nine days to dry. I wanted to use that time to paint.

When I mixed the pigments with the linseed oil and varnish, at varying consistencies, I always had the same problem—it either was too thick or became translucent. I painted a self-portrait, but the

---

2   Animal protein used for painting should not smell. If it smells, it is a sign that the glue has gone rancid and will probably crack or flake. This glue was smelly because I didn't have access to high-quality protein.
3   Rancid linen was also a favorite treat of insects.

next time, I tried to somehow improve on the technique.

After warming up the glue protein for that first coat, it wasn't transparent like the oil or the varnish. Still, I thought this cloudy beige liquid was better than the egg yolk[4] I learned they had used in Europe long ago. I thought perhaps mixing the marble dust with the rabbit-skin glue might save the one step that took so much time to dry.

The marble dust mixed well with the glue, and I was surprised that if I was careful about the amount of marble I added, the mixture would be not only liquid but also opaque!

It went on smoothly with the brush and dried as soon as the water evaporated. This was a fantastic and totally unexpected find. I realized that the glue was coating and binding the fine grains of marble together while also adhering it to the linen.

I thought that if it could happen with the marble dust, it would also be possible with the various powdered chemical pigments I had.

It worked!

I was a little bit closer to painting in my ideal way. I would be able to use lines as I hadn't been able to do before. And the paint would be strong without blending or thinning. I felt a freedom of expression I hadn't enjoyed before.

To make the lines go thicker or thinner as I pulled the paint across the linen, it worked well by twisting flat brushes. I had done this before with house paint on sheets for the drama backdrops. But I was worried about how permanent it was. The chemical pigments didn't instill confidence, but they were the best that was available.

---

4   Egg yolk is also an animal protein. Surprisingly, it becomes transparent when it dries.

This was my brilliant discovery. And with it, I hoped the beauty I created could change the art world forever.

I knew that once I became a professional artist, I would have to paint using materials that were as permanent as an art collector had a right to expect. If what I had to say was important enough for me to spend a long time making the paint and working on the painting, it was important that it last long enough for the message to arrive. I was sorry to learn that Van Gogh couldn't afford better-quality paint. His paintings have begun to fade, and we are no longer able to see how they looked when he painted them. I didn't want that with my work.

At the time, I didn't know that fooling around with art supplies like this would change the course of my life forever. I just reveled in the joy of exploration and experimentation.

———————

One of these experimental paintings I painted as a high school senior was accepted to a juried gallery show behind the Phillips Collection. I was afraid this new medium might eventually crack or flake. So, when asked the selling price, I said it was not for sale.

At the opening, a woman in Kelly green grilled me about my materials and techniques. I was pleased that she showed an interest. The matte surface of the paint was what stood out to her. What had I used? How had it been done? Then she said something that changed the course of my life. She said she thought a similar technique may already have been used in Japan for a long time. With this one comment, the built-up excitement of exhibiting artwork created with this new technique of mine came crashing down around me.

How could this be? Did my brilliant discovery already exist somewhere? I didn't want to believe it. It was only later that I realized the importance of that information. If the Japanese had been using a similar technique for a long time, it was likely they also had pigments that last.

I knew only that I was painting plant life with a freedom I had never before enjoyed.

7

GAMBLING WITH MY FUTURE

As graduation approached, I couldn't escape the question: where should I study after high school? I had thought about a few art schools, but my father was dead set against it.

"Art is a hobby, not a career," he said.

I was to choose almost anything but art.

But there was nothing else I wanted to do. This had been my plan since I was eight. And having dedicated myself to art as I had, this seemed like the logical next step. The stern resistance I had from my father came as a surprise. This was the one thing I could not yield, and yet it also meant a horrible confrontation. In the end, my maternal grandmother came to my rescue. She reminded him of his youthful dreams of becoming a forest ranger. Just as he was given a chance at it, shouldn't I also be allowed to at least make an attempt? He couldn't argue with that. I owe an immense debt to my grandmother for this saving intervention. Her favorite flowers often appear in my paintings as a tribute.

Finally, my father agreed, but on two critical conditions—that I should apply to only the best university that also had an art program, not an arts college, and if I was not accepted, that I should give up my dream of being an artist. Though the risk was enormous, I could see what he said was true. This was the ultimate gamble. I had been so fully invested in art that I didn't have an alternate plan. My concerned father often talked of the risk of putting all my eggs in one basket. But my strategy had been that only through laser-like focus was I going to be able to make my plan work. Failure was not an option. I was under enough pressure that I couldn't allow myself to wonder, What if I'm not accepted? He wanted me to aim high. But which university was the best? We decided the arbiter, and final authority, should be Dr. Taylor, the director of the National Collection of Fine Arts.

The idea of approaching Dr. Taylor was daunting. Though I had worked there for three years, I'd never met him. I pictured Dr. Taylor ruling from a cloud over the Acropolis on which the Greek temple of the museum was situated. I suspected he was the imposing man I had sometimes passed in the marble halls.

When I knocked on his door, my suspicions were confirmed.

Dr. Taylor thanked me for working on Vice President and Mrs. Mondale's exhibition.[5] Then in answer to my question about the best university, he said, "Oh, that would be College of Fine Arts."

---

5   During the administration of President Jimmy Carter, Vice President Walter Mondale and his wife, Joan Adams Mondale, had already been collecting art for years and actively participated in the art world. They brought a portion of their collection to their Washington, DC, residence at the United States Naval Observatory, which was featured in the exhibition titled *Art from the Vice President's House.*

I learned that was how his generation referred to Carnegie Mellon University in Pittsburgh. Suddenly, the stakes were higher. I had heard the rumor that only one applicant out of 50 was accepted to their art program.

I sent for the application. Fifty works would be required at the interview. I could pick all similar works, which could prove focus and mastery. Or I could choose a variety, which might show innovation. I chose the latter. We stuffed our station wagon with paintings, ink drawings, many sketchbooks, and studies of nudes I had done at the Corcoran Museum School. I couldn't fit in the backdrops I'd painted for stage productions. On a whim, I added a ceramic end table I'd made.

I assumed a painting professor would critique my work. Instead, I was interviewed by Professor Eberle, who headed the ceramics department.

He looked surprised when he saw the pile of sketchbooks and said, "Normally, we count each page, not each sketchbook separately. Nobody ever brings this much."

He told me they had a great ceramics department and were looking for innovative artists for his program. He eyed my end table. Turning it around slowly, he said, "We sure would like to have you in the program."

I wanted to be a painter, and here I was being recruited for ceramics. What was the right thing to say in this situation?

I went with *thank you.*

8

QUESTIONING MODERNISM

visited the mailbox multiple times a day. Over and over, I reviewed the interview in my mind. It hadn't gone as I anticipated, and that scared me. I found it impossible to focus on anything. Drawing was a distraction, but as I look over the sketchbooks of that time, all I see is the stress of twisted and deformed figures in a heavy dark space.

After agonizing weeks of waiting, a letter of acceptance came. Dad was surprised. I think that may have been the first time he saw how my art stood in others' estimation. "Well, a deal is a deal," he conceded. His initial bit of advice was that if for any reason I felt like changing my major, that would be fine with him.

I felt lucky to be one of the 90 people accepted to our freshman class, but the workload was such that just catching a cold could make a student fall too far behind to ever catch up. Before winter break, they named which students were not invited to return. By the end of four years, only 15 of us remained to graduate.

In addition to the other classes we were taking, life-drawing classes under Professor Olds could add up to as much as nine hours a day. The human body was so familiar to us that we could tell instinctively when it was drawn wrong. This was a good way to train the eye and the hand.

Skinny men were the easiest. You could see the bones and the muscles right there. We drew a ninety-year-old woman who had been a fan dancer in the 1920s. There was even a pregnant woman. We were supposed to see what the lumps in her stomach suggested. Where were the baby's knees? The elbows? I remember the gasp of the entire class as we watched the baby shift inside.

The model's union requires that no model pose for more than 20 minutes without a break. That meant we needed to develop the skill to finish our drawings of each pose within 20 minutes.

Most of the slides shown in art history class were already familiar to me. The research project I chose for art history was most interesting. I wanted to get at the origins of modernism and the beginnings of abstraction.

I found that Whistler had been an arbiter of taste for the latter part of the 19th century, and his innovative design influences home interiors to this day. Whistler was an American who lived and worked in London. But his greatest influence was Japan.

He was thought to have painted the first truly modern painting, an abstraction called *Nocturne in Black and Gold: The Falling Rocket*. This was like a Rosetta stone but for art. It was pure abstraction, while at the same time, it contained the transcendent beauty of Whistler's aesthetic.

I also learned something else that year. Contemporary artists at that time in America were considered outsiders. Political leaders treated art as unethical or against social norms. I couldn't understand how artists of that time would embrace that role and even celebrate their positions as outsiders. It had always been my assumption that if possible, my art was to be an influence for good. I couldn't imagine how I would work in such an environment.

During that semester, my painting professor, Sam Gilliam, challenged me over the materials I was using. It was the technique I had invented in high school, and he told me that because it wasn't permanent, I needed to switch to oils or acrylics. I tried to persuade him that it was in fact permanent. He offered a challenge. If I could pour a pitcher of water down the front of one of my six-foot-tall canvasses without harming it, he would concede. We went to my studio, and I put the painting at an angle and poured all the water straight down. The painting was fine. This was proper assurance. But I knew by the lightfastness ratings on the chemical pigments I was using that Professor Gilliam could easily challenge the permanence of my art once again.[6]

---

6   Sam Gilliam is a special hero of mine, and I felt privileged to be chosen by him to participate in his classes. His innovative paintings advanced the work of Morris Louis, Kenneth Noland, and Gene Davis. The overall field of color was a painting style of the 1950s and '60s in Washington, DC, known as the Washington Color School. Sam made an international name for himself when he took paintings off their supports, draping and suspending them to create works that were simultaneously sculptural and pictographic.

9

Hay There, What Happened to Your Permanence?

If it is worth making, it is worth making well. If it is worth making well, it is worth making to last. Art requires a lot of effort, so it needs to be worth it.

While at Carnegie Mellon, I visited the Carnegie Museum of Art regularly. As with the Smithsonian, I became familiar with the paintings on display. The continued exposure gave me a sense of what captures and maintains interest. Some paintings revealed a new facet with each succeeding viewing. Others made an impact at first, but when seen time and again, the initial interest turned out to be the result of gimmickry.

A painting by the German contemporary neo-Expressionist artist Anselm Kiefer hung on the wall while I was there. As with many of his paintings at the time, tar had been raked onto the surface of the canvas, and hay was pressed into the tar. Every time I passed it, more bits of hay had fallen on the floor.

The guard saw me staring at the fallen straw and said, "The thing sheds like a dog. There's more every day. At this rate, by the end of the year, there won't be anything left."

I thought of the money necessary to purchase this painting. An art restorer told me her concern was for the owners of similar paintings. Did they know how high-maintenance these paintings were? She said paintings might be valued at tens of millions of dollars, and the preservation work could also cost in the millions.

I mentioned how this was nothing new. The Renaissance historian Vasari wrote on the deteriorating condition of Leonardo da Vinci's *Last Supper*. The art restorer agreed, and I asked whether other Renaissance paintings have also become increasingly difficult to preserve and restore.

That same woman said it was not the case. She explained artists had been concerned with the endurance of their work until around the 1950s. After that time, we began to see a disregard for the physical and chemical requirements of a painting.

The worst by far that she had ever personally seen were some Jackson Pollock paintings. He had used house paint on raw canvas. Not only did the oil in the paint weaken the canvas fibers, but they also degraded so badly that the whole structure of the painting was in jeopardy—and the colors of the house paint had faded to an alarming degree.

In the 1950s, new pigments and mediums had been developed. Acrylic paints had come on the scene without a serious history. How long would they last? The question remains to this day.

Many artists focus solely on the content of their work and blithely wave off any concern for permanence. Imagine a masterpiece for which the content is universal and timeless, yet for preventable reasons, it may not stand the test of time.

I remembered the opening of an exhibition when I was in high school. The woman in bright Kelly green spoke of permanence in connection with Japanese art. Could the solution to my problem be found in Japan?

While at Carnegie Mellon University, if ever I heard the word *beautiful*, it was uttered with a sneer. This came as a shock to me. The whole aim of my art was to create a thing of enduring beauty.

As far as I could tell, the goal of everyone within the art world was to become famous and "hit it big." The idea was to push boundaries and break taboos in the name of freedom of expression, however they interpreted it. By causing outrage in society's more prudish ranks, an artist could aspire to having bankable name recognition.

But I didn't see that as a sustainable way to polish the skills I hoped to cultivate. Nor could I see a career with that as my goal.

I had heard the story of someone who had his grant proposal accepted by a prestigious endowment. He felt he had made it big. Knowing he was on the cusp of great things, he used that money to buy a flashy car; however, upon completing the work, he received almost no recognition and no further prospects. He sold the car at a loss.

At the time, there was no available instruction on the business of being an artist. It was all about technique. The idea was that the better artists we were, the more likely we would be recognized. It was only a mercenary artist who spent time on the business. At the time, self-promotion by the artist was beyond the pale.

Artists were creating works calculated to elicit extreme reactions. One social issue could fuel decades of artistic activity. The words of an angry politician were enough to ensure an enterprising artist a long career of notoriety and relative economic stability.

The temptation to take that route was strong, but by doing so, I might handcuff myself to that image in people's minds forever.

This was the situation in the art world as I knew it. It made the makeshift studio of my childhood seem small. But in shedding that older shell, I found myself in a larger but wholly uncomfortable world.

Too often Professor Olds labeled my out-of-class assignments with the pejorative *pretty*. Unfortunately, as the school year progressed, it was clear that for art to be worthwhile, it had to be modern or edgy—to make the observer ill at ease. This was the opposite of what I had aimed for, and I wondered if I could resist the pressure. If I pursued *my* idea of beauty, would I not be invited to return next semester?

It felt wrong to adjust my work merely to win the praise of my professors. If I abandoned my goals, the joy would evaporate. If I should be dismissed, I couldn't return. If they were going to eliminate me, I didn't know what I'd do. After working so hard to get in, if I were to be kicked out, that would be the end of art for me. I knew my father would not give me a second chance.

Gone was the rewarding feeling I had as a child, of making things that pleased people. Now it seemed the goal was to create something strong, imposing, or overly assertive. It needed to be ironic, critical, or cynical.

It all seemed unnecessarily negative. I could see how upperclass-men were gradually hardened into these expressions of modernity, and I couldn't see myself doing that for the rest of my life just to fit in.

10

I NEVER WANT TO SEE
YOUR FACE AGAIN

needed to know if this education would get me to where I wanted to go as a painter. During my first Thanksgiving break, I saw my earlier paintings through different eyes. Remembering the encouragement I had received as an eight-year-old, I decided to meet with Dr. Telford again. I trusted him to give me sound advice.

I immediately wrote down his words as a record I could refer to, and after sincere reflection, I knew I had received the very advice I needed to hear: "Make your profession in life one of giving and not self-serving. Communicate a message of love, not contention. Strive to understand the background of the people you serve, and they'll respond with love and understanding."

Even though I can practically repeat it from memory, I have kept that paper and still look at it from time to time. It has continued to guide me.

Hoping a new perspective might help me think through this dilemma, I decided on something risky: I would take some time off from school.

I knew of a program where one could live abroad for very little money. I could teach English and a little about American culture and experience life in a foreign country. I knew others who had gone to various countries, and it sounded like a worthwhile experience. Perhaps I would learn that foreign language I had missed in high school. Any place was as good as any other. What was more important, it would get me out of my head. I needed some distance—to evaluate my feelings on modernism—and my own expression.

I had made a little money mowing lawns and selling prints, and Dad paid for the rest. When signing up for the program, I had no idea where I might be sent.

After taking the language-aptitude test in the spring, I was told I had tied for the highest score. I hoped that might bode well for my placement.

During the nervous two months of waiting for my assignment, I made friends with the other high scorer, Brett Scharffs. By surprising coincidence, Brett was assigned to the same country.

Japan. What remarkable luck!

Just before learning which students would be cut, I told Professor Olds I would not be returning in the fall. I had learned I was going to Japan. Perhaps I could learn how to make my paintings permanent, as I had been told the Japanese might have done for centuries.

He was furious. He said he had been so critical of my work because he thought it held promise and that leaving school at such a time in my development would absolutely ruin the progress I had made.

He said he never wanted to see my face again.

Before leaving, Brett Scharffs and I got together to study what we could of the language. With a set of handmade flash cards and two hours, we alternately wielded the cards and memorized them. We learned all the 46-hiragana syllabary.[7] In retrospect, it seems surprising, but it happened.

I was assigned to work on Shikoku, the smallest of the four main islands of Japan. Perhaps, while I was there, I could learn more about the art materials and techniques I thought I had invented years ago. I wondered how much language study would be necessary before I could find someone who could show me.

In July of 1982, I packed my bags with plenty of empty sketchbooks and went to Japan.

---

7   This syllabary is a set of written characters that represent syllables of sounds—usually in consonant vowel pairs. The Japanese writing system is comprised of kanji characters and two syllabaries— hiragana and katakana. Kanji characters were adopted from China. Katakana is used mainly for borrowed foreign words.

11

IN THE TRENCHES

My arrival was met with the smell of tobacco smoke and pomade. Narita airport was a nerve-jangling experience. It was like a scene in a war movie.

We were loaded into camouflage buses with steel bars on the windows. Shoddily built huts and watchtowers dotted the barren landscape. As the bus wove between berms and trenches, I wondered if they were the remains of the Second World War.

On our way to the nearest station, a man in combat attire stopped us and boarded the bus. He carried the first gun I had ever seen in real life. It was strapped to his back, and the butt showed up behind his shoulder. He glared at each of us, checked our passports at gunpoint, and compared our faces with the photos.

Not understanding either the written or spoken language meant a lot of my earliest impressions of Japan, though vivid, were confused.

It wouldn't be until later that I fully understood what I had seen.

The land used for the airport had been requisitioned by the government from farmers, for a pittance. The farmers were fighting desperately for rightful compensation.[8]

When the bus finally arrived at the station, nothing seemed awry in the least. In Tokyo, everything was clean. In fact, the jumble and activity were amazing. Such ordered chaos as we saw in the city could be attained only by a consciously chosen harmony.

We arrived in Okayama and met our supervisors. After an interview, the area manager decided to have me teach in the school in Marugame on the island of Shikoku. They took us out to dinner, where we had pork cutlets, or *tonkatsu*. I bought some aerogram papers and wrote home to say, "Tonkatsu is delicious."

I was given detailed instructions on how to take the ferry, where to transfer to the train, and what time it would arrive at Zentsuji Station. There I would meet my direct supervisor, who would also be my teaching companion. He would explain everything so that I could eventually teach as well. I was counting on learning Japanese as I taught.

When the time came, I arrived at Zentsuji Station. It was a little wooden structure the size of a small house. Short weeds cropped up between the ties of its two tracks. The trainer assigned to me met me there, and he was Japanese.

The room where we were to live was at the end of a series of row houses on the side of a narrow road. An expanse of rice paddies

8   The names and faces of these farmers were pinned to the walls of train stations and post offices. They staged a decades-long terrorist operation that lasted until the '90s, when the government compensated them at a fair price. Narita airport is considered Tokyo's international airport, though it is situated in the neighboring prefecture of Chiba.

stretched out behind. There was not so much as a curb separating the pavement and the two and a half feet down to the green blades of rice planted in water and soft mud. It would require skill to walk along here. Should a car come the other way, I might not have a place to stand.

I was shown where to take off my shoes. Once inside, an acrid smell assaulted me, and my roommate asked if I could squat without falling over.

"Like this," he said and showed me a deep squat.

I was puzzled. What on earth did that have to do with anything? I was not so limber. Though I could squat, my heels came up, and I teetered on my toes.

"That won't do," he said. "You're up too high and much too unsteady."

Was this some sort of initiation? I understood when he introduced me to the toilet. The "honorable latrine" was the defining feature of the apartment. It was an oblong hole in the floor surrounded by a gleaming white porcelain edging, under which a pit of unknowable depth sank into darkness. I assumed other teachers had gone through all this as well.[9]

He then prepared dinner. Knowing that I was an American, he gave me an immense helping. I was tired and jet lagged and, due to the aforementioned odor, not particularly hungry. But as I watched the tofu sauce slither down the mountain of rice, I felt the pressure of his unspoken words: I made it for you.

---

9   Even at the time, the average Japanese person would consider our plumbing shocking. As this was my first time in Japan, I didn't realize our plumbing was decades behind the times. My replacement knew enough to alert the head office to the issue and find more hygienic, if less economical housing. After that, all my rooming arrangements had proper plumbing.

When I had eaten a third of the way through it, I was more than done. But he said, "Each grain of rice is a bead of farmer's sweat." He complained about my being a messy eater and insisted I must not leave so much as one grain.

Luckily, I had had a long day and fell asleep on an available futon before I was forced to finish.

I was awakened the next morning by a pungent stench in my nose. It was from the "defining feature," and the smell saturated the futon, the pillow, my suitcase, and my clothing. The first errand we had that day was grocery shopping. I was glad for the opportunity to be away from the fumes.

––––––––––

I needed to learn to shop and cook with the ingredients available in the Maruyoshi Center supermarket in Zentsuji. I expected the money we sent to open an account would be available any day at the Taiyokobemitsui Ginko Bank. Unfortunately, I had only the cash I had exchanged at the airport.

While I was going down the grocery store aisle, a woman caught sight of me. Upon seeing my face, she dropped a carton of eggs in shock at such an unexpected sight. With this, I learned that to the Japanese, taller people with more pronounced facial features than theirs can be frightening.

I picked out a grapefruit, and my trainer put it back.

"Teachers don't eat fruit. Too expensive." He indicated two on-ions, a head of cabbage, and a two-for-one bag of noodles with a bonus packet of spice mix as something more economical.

At the time, a hundred dollars would exchange to about 24,000 yen. I bought two large meals' worth of food for the bargain price of 60 cents.[10]

I saw that living in Japan could be inexpensive. I stored it away in my memory and thought about what it might take to start out here as an artist. It would be better than waiting tables in New York. But I didn't want to get scurvy from avoiding fruit in deference to my trainer.

10 That was a little less than the cost of one grapefruit.

MINKY MOMO

I *would need some way to get around so* I could make the daily trips to teach in Marugame, a 50-minute bike ride away. We would have taken the train, but that was also an expense we could ill afford.

A man taking my English class offered me a bicycle his daughter had outgrown. I agreed, thinking it couldn't hurt to take a look. When he brought it around, my heart sank.

It was lavender with pink plastic streamers spewing from the ends of the handles. *Minky MoMo* was written on both sides, and a saccharine pink girl with bubbly eyes was depicted in more than one place.

My knees cleared the handlebars as I pedaled, even after I raised the seat as high as it would go.

Every day, I stopped by the ATM, hoping my deposit had registered in my bank account. Riding Minky MoMo pretty much did away with my pride. I kept telling myself, This is only temporary until I can afford a real one.

I felt completely removed from the things that gave me joy—plants, birds, flowers, and most of all, painting. On top of that, it was frustrating always wondering what was going on. Being illiterate was hard. But most of all, the bondage of being illiterate was a much harder experience than learning such a difficult language. I no longer took the freedom of reading for granted.

I found a good dictionary. *Sanseido's Daily Concise,* with its onionskin pages of minute print, fit into my back pocket, and the soft cover soon fit the contour of my rear end. I became rather quick on the draw. Within moments of hearing a word, I was on it, lest I forget what it was before looking it up.

Knowing the hiragana syllabary became essential. It was phonetic. So, if I could remember the order of the 46 symbols, I would be able to look up a word. The key was finding a memorable concept to match the shape of the letter, which could also be reminiscent of its sound. It was a little like drawing wings, a stinger, and stripes on the letter B.

The greatest difficulty with looking up words was that they were not written with a space in between. Sometimes it became hard to know where a word started. For instance, if one didn't know what the word was and saw it all mashed in with other strings of letters, separating the words could be tricky. For example, *Sometimessimpleaccidentsamuse* might be separated as, "So met I mess I'm pleacc I dent Sam use." This is where I would jump to my dictionary and fruitlessly look up *pleacc.* Eventually, I became familiar with enough words and their contexts that it was easier to know where they began and ended.

Then it was a matter of using my visual memory to learn the complex kanji that represent concepts. There would usually be two, but sometimes five or more, ways of reading each character.

The order and direction of each stroke needed to be memorized for each kanji, because of their subtle architecture of space and balance. The more complicated the characters, the more essential the proper arrangement of lines became, especially when writing speedily.

DIFFERENT—NOT WRONG

The way I always did things in the States wasn't necessarily the right way in Japan. I learned that through experience.

At a train station, I once asked the ticket taker about a train, and he snapped the answer at me with obvious irritation. Apparently, by folding my arms, he thought I was rudely expressing impatience.

Another time, after helping someone carry a box of books, I dusted off my hands in the way we customarily express *Well, that's that.* Clearly, the person I had helped was incensed. I found out Japanese people interpret that gesture as disgust with doing a dirty task. It meant "I want nothing more to do with that." I learned the hard way that, by asking questions, I could prevent embarrassing misunderstandings.

On my second night in Zentsuji, I was no longer exhausted. But I was unable to sleep, because the sewage smell had seeped into the bedding and was impossible to ignore. The subtle movements of the steamy night air caused the glass in the door of our latrine to shift and ring out as a constant reminder of the invading vapors. I got up in the night and wedged a knife in the gap to silence it.

The overwhelming smell of the latrine occupied my every thought. I asked my roommate if it would be all right if I fashioned a lid out of cardboard to keep the smell at bay.

"Good idea. The guy before you broke the porcelain lid, and we haven't had anything to replace it."

Maybe stoicism wouldn't be necessary if creativity could fix the situation.

Our one naked light bulb showed the squalor of our room in stark detail. By cutting a hole in the bottom of a tin can, I turned it into a spotlight for the low table that served as our only piece of furniture. My inexpertly cooked food somehow looked better in that light.

The third morning, as I dripped in the heat, I sat at my desk to study. To catch a breeze, I opened the back window to the rice paddy while I studied Japanese.

As I was studying in my undershirt, the light from the window dimmed. I wondered whether there would be a storm that day. Looking up, I noticed a crowd of elementary school children had filled up the window, peering at me in silent curiosity. I was embarrassed to be seen by so many and at such close range while still in my underwear.

I slid the window closed, whereupon the children came around to the front, opened the door, and stepped inside.

"Good morning!" They had been assaulted by only my upper half at the window, but now they experienced the rest of me on display.

Stunned, I sat stock still. I had never felt less privacy. However, reluctant to lose such enthusiastic fans, I replied, "Ohayo!" (*Good morning*, in Japanese.)

They took off their hats and bowed in turn until the final one closed the door. This was one of many experiences where a person's curiosity overpowered their respect for privacy.

It took many attempts with confused questions, but I finally learned that the vestibule where the shoes remain is considered outdoors to the Japanese. Before they step up into any dwelling, they will open the door, step in, and then announce their presence. The area just inside the vestibule usually has a frosted glass door or a slotted curtain to create a little privacy between that and the living quarters—and to prevent that kind of surprise. We had no such curtain.

I spent a lot of those early months that way, not fully understanding what was going on and just trying to learn about cultural differences.

Nothing could have prepared me for the new and surprising experiences I would have in Japan. For the first time, I met university students who felt perfectly comfortable saying they made models of things with toothpicks, collected erasers shaped like animals, or had other hobbies that seemed unusual to me.

Based on my experiences in America, I expected to hear about cars, sports-related hobbies, or popular music. Although Japanese society expects such things as courtesy and a polite awareness of others, private issues are left entirely to the individual. Being cool doesn't seem as important to them. Fitting in doesn't mean being the same.

Museum attendance is high, and classical music is popular. Everyone seems to know art, to some degree. Unlike the average American, most Japanese have a ready answer when asked what artists they like. I also found to my surprise and joy that artists are well respected as an essential part of society. This remains true even today.

In Japan, I witnessed a freedom of expression that, to me, was completely new and liberating. People had the confidence to appreciate whatever art appealed to them.

It was an unexpected pleasure.

Nevertheless, in Zentsuji, I was unable to find an art supply store with anything but Western-style paint and art supplies.

In a cramped storefront, it took all I knew of the language to describe what I was looking for. When asking if they had any animal protein, the seller looked confused and raised his hands in protest.

Here I was, at the other end of the world, looking for something no one seemed to have heard of. He asked, "Why are you here? You should go to the butcher for animal protein."

I left empty handed.

14

FIVE MOUNTAINS

I **was better prepared for my next visit to** an art supply store. My dictionary said the word for pigment was *ganryo*. I found a shop in the central arcade in the larger town of Marugame. I parked Minky MoMo and entered. As I did, the shopkeeper wore that familiar look on his face. He was thinking, Oh no, a foreigner!

I would be as polite as I knew how to be. Did they have any *ganryo*?

"No, not in a town like this. You're a Westerner, right? Why don't you just use *your own* paints? Paints in a tube, ready to use. That's the only kind I can sell here.

"We have artists we call the Five Mountains of Nihonga. Their names are Higashiyama, Hirayama, Kayama, Sugiyama, and Takayama. But you have great artists at home. Why would you want to come all the way here, when you have Picasso and Van Gogh?"

They only had oil paints. I had come so far, and yet it seemed I was no closer to learning more about this specific painting technique.

At that point, I could find only oil paints. I bought tubes of burnt umber, raw umber, ocher, and white, plus a brush. I found a little free time to paint a self-portrait on a scrap of plywood by using the mirror in an outbuilding.

Much later, after gaining greater fluency, I learned only a small number of artists are especially particular about their pigments and binders. These people are called nihonga artists, and they use exactly what I had experimented with and was looking for. The vast majority of artists in Japan are heavily influenced by Western painters. As a Western artist trying to learn art techniques in Japan, I find it ironic that Japanese artists are looking to the West. Western art has an aura of coolness and sophistication that professional artists and hobbyists long for. The traditional materials are hard to find.[11]

I made a discovery. I was told the few stores that carried the kind of supplies I wanted were only in Tokyo and perhaps Kyoto. I realized the word *nihonga* was key. That word was met with a pause of respect, surprise, and skepticism.

---

11 According to *Bijutsu no Mado*, there are approximately 680 art supply stores in Japan. Of those, I have only been able to find 10 that specialize in the traditional Nihonga materials.

15

THE UPPER CRUST
DRESSES FOR DINNER

As the days continued, the bank in Japan still hadn't verified my transfer. I shouldn't have spent that money on the paints. But it had been so long. And I didn't even care that it was oil paint.

A month passed, and I was out of ready cash. My roommate said if I went to the bakery, I could probably beg for their cast-off bread crusts. But only if I said they were for my dog. I must be sure to dress in a suit and tie to act as if I didn't need them for myself.

I got a lot of practice at using what I could find in the kitchen. A little *usuta sosu* (Worcestershire sauce) at the bottom of a frying pan and some stir-fried crusts with a sprinkle of soy sauce became quite a delicacy.

I scrounged some cooking oil and cinnamon sugar to make crunchy cinnamon breadcrust sticks for dessert. A bit of milk and an egg made French toast strips. The crust side wasn't absorbent, and it only soaked into one side, allowing the batter to stretch further.

I got my first letter from home and discovered an airmail aerogram took nine days to arrive. Even if a reply was instantaneously returned, that would take another nine days.

The letter from my parents said, "We found a place that serves Japanese food and tried a variety of things on the menu. Everything was absolutely tonkatsu!"

After a month like this, my roommate/supervisor left to return to school. His replacement was an American—a rather quiet person whose Japanese was quite good. He spent a lot of time studying his well-used dictionary and kept mostly to himself. I wasn't sure why he was there. I was glad for everything my supervisor had shown me, because I had to take over most of the teaching.

The second month was when it suddenly struck me what I had committed to, and 18 months of this seemed insurmountable. I remember looking up at the moon and reminding myself that that very same moon would be seen by people I love in a few hours. I spent that month trying to get acclimated.

I tried to focus on why I was there, but the one thing I wished I could forget was the latrine. Each day, I faced it with increasing disgust. The contents of the tank rose dramatically, and I did not want to see the level rise any more. I came to a sudden realization. The porcelain object in the corner must be the urinal, and the bar thing you push up that releases the water must be how you flush it.

It was obvious now that we should have been using the urinal instead of having everything collect in one place. After that discovery, the rising tide in the porcelain tank slowed somewhat.

16

VIOLENT RACING TRIBE

O*ne night, as we returned from teaching,* we were surrounded by a *Bosozoku* motorcycle gang (literally translated as "Violent Racing Tribe"). Four of them surrounded us. They had slicked-back hair, headbands, and tightly cinched leather jackets with words written in an especially spiky style. They wore red, orange, and purple pants that were wide below the thighs and knees and tied in at the ankles. They wore plastic toilet slippers like the ones public venues supply for use in their restrooms.

I was completely nonplussed. Through rotten teeth, they spat out what I assumed were epithets and menacing phrases. Not understanding any of it, I searched in vain through my pocket dictionary. It made our exchange particularly unsatisfactory, if not totally galling for this gang.

One character with red pants had an aluminum baseball bat that made a metallic sound as he dragged it. "Orah! Minky MoMo jan!" he said as he ran it under the pink tassels of my bicycle.

It was met with whoops of laughter from the others. One word was a particular source of mirth, and they used it quite a bit. I later learned saying it to a police officer could get one arrested.

Our complete ignorance was our saving grace. We appeared to be unflappable. Somehow, we were able to make it through the exchange with an extremely simple and formal *Good evening to you all,* which I suppose they thought was hilarious and, at the same time, sufficiently respectful.

Heavy, warm raindrops fell, threatening a squall. With knees spread wide, the gang quickly remounted their motors and left in a roar of chromium horsepower and unmuffled fumes.

We still had 20 minutes more to go before reaching safety and dry clothes. As my roommate pushed ahead into the distance, I struggled to control my emotions. Thunder roared at the face of the mountains, then lightning cracked all around. I reached into my almost-depleted reserves for some comfort.

The only thing that came to me were the words to a hymn. It was mostly for me, but I didn't care if God heard it. My exhausted legs pumped, speeding the tempo. I half shouted and half sang in defiance, as close as I could remember the words.

Lead, kindly light, amid the encircling gloom,
Lead thou me on!
The night is dark, and I am far from home,
Lead thou me on!
I loved the garish day in spite of fears,

Pride ruled my will, remember not past tears![12]

That night, on returning to our place, I got out the cooking knife and lopped off the pink tassels of my Minky MoMo.

I have since learned most of these gangs are where dropouts collect, eventually graduating to be recruited as the *chimpira* toadies of the *yakuza* crime syndicates. Their slippers were trophies of their petty larcenies, and the teeth were a result of losing enamel from sniffing paint thinner to get high.

12 John Henry Newman, "The Pillar of the Cloud," *The British Magazine and Monthly Register*, 1834. Text by John Henry Newman (1801–1890). Music by John B. Dykes (1823–1876). I love the fact that this is Mahatma Gandhi's favorite hymn.

DISCOMMODED

The next day, we reached a critical point. The latrine would soon overflow. The acrid humidity of the summer's nights had increased. Heavy currents of air flowed from the back room and gathered pungency when passing over the roiling hole.

I discussed it with my roommate. He had never lived in a place like this and wasn't equipped to even imagine what was to be done.

I was desperate. I realized if *we* had such a disaster, surely our neighbors in the row house would be contending with similar issues.

I prepared all the words that I expected to need, rehearsed them in my mind, and knocked on the door of the neighbor to our left.

A woman in her 30s came out and said, partly with gestures and in a stew of English and Japanese, that we were supposed to call the truck. They would come around and take care of it. Holding her nose, she indicated that she had also been aware of the smell. "Oh, and whatever you do, don't forget about the water," she said. "That is essential. They don't like it if you don't give them enough water."

She gave me the telephone number to call, and we went to the phone booth in the next block. This would be my first experience with a telephone in Japan.

I put in my 10-yen coin and dialed the number. It rang, but when the voice answered, it was interrupted by a buzz. I spoke my piece, and just as the man tried to explain the problem with the phone, it went dead.

Had he hung up on me? Perhaps he just didn't have the patience to figure out what I was saying. I had written down all his words I didn't understand. He hadn't sounded angry.

I refused to give up. I had had enough of the gross fixture in the corner of our room. Whatever it took, I would make it disappear. I was going to overcome my timidity, ignorance of social situations, and fear of communicating incorrectly. Again, I refined my notes and reviewed the vocabulary I would need.

Subject, *I*. Object, *toilet*. Verb, *overflow*. I dialed one more time, and the phone connected immediately.

The voice was drawing on his high school English. "More money in. More!"

I put all the 10-yen coins I had into the phone, and the excess fell into the catcher. As I spoke, I could hear the coins clink into the pile of coins inside, and the sound added to the pressure.

The man was patient as I thumbed through the dictionary. At times, I miraculously came up with a word I had heard only in passing or in an unrelated context. I had the phone sandwiched between my cheek and shoulder as I wrote down the words. My roommate pitched in to keep the dialogue going.

In the end, I grasped the situation. The truck man had just been there a few days ago. He made his rounds the third Thursday of every month, so we would have to wait until next month. I told him we couldn't wait. It would be too late in a day or two. He said it would cost extra for a special trip.

I thanked him profusely. As I did, my words flowed freely in a way I had never experienced before. I expressed both my frustration and my tentative gratitude with fluency.

Had I just made a breakthrough? I looked down at my scribbled notes. Yes, and I would control my own destiny by learning all I could. I was determined never again to feel like a victim.

My basic need to survive had overtaken any concern for the permanency of art materials. I was stuck. I would have to wait with the hope of going to Tokyo someday, which I was told was the one and only place such supplies could be found.

Until the day appointed for our man's arrival, we spent as much time as possible anywhere else and made certain to "empty ourselves" at every opportunity. He was to arrive at our place at three in the afternoon the day after tomorrow. Even so, it was dicey. We had to cancel a teaching session just to meet the man with the truck.

I wasn't sure what to expect but found the process much more pleasant than I had imagined. A tank truck rolled up, and the man got out in a rubberized jumpsuit. He pointed to the floor-level window and asked me to open it. For reasons of privacy, I had never thought to leave it open. He pulled out a duct-sized hose and carefully maneuvered it into the window. The driver of the truck turned on the vacuum mechanism. All the excitement brought out our neighbor, who looked on as well.

It took longer than the man had expected. It was a hot day, and he was sweating in his rubber suit. Now for the water. I offered him a tall glass of cold water to drink.

He waved it away. "No, not to drink. I need buckets!"

The neighbor looked at me as if to say *I told you so*. But she then generously supplied her own bucket, which she filled from a spigot outside. It took three loads of water to clean out the basin, which was soon porcelain white and shining.

The man pointed to something with his rubber gloves. There were yellowed grains of rice in a groove between the wall of our room and the pavement.

"See that hole?" he explained. "That's where the water comes out from your kitchen sink."

I was horrified. Now I understood more than I wished. I realized why my former Japanese roommate had used netting in the sink. It was for catching all the uneaten particles from the dishes he washed. There on display in this groove, in front of the entire neighborhood, was the crudity of these offensive Americans.

How unsanitary we had been! I was disgusted with my insensitivity. I had assumed everything would just be whooshed away and disappear underground.

Why hadn't I noticed earlier?

We paid him, and he said, "I've given you two months' worth of vacuuming for free." He brought the change over to my roommate, who looked at me—to add half of it to the running tab of money I already owed him.

The man left, and our neighbor said if there was anything we didn't understand or any questions we had, we must feel free to ask her.

The now-normal smell of the place gave me indescribable joy. We could even enjoy dinner! And there was no hazard involved in taking a big drink of water, which I did freely. I then took advantage of the increased capacity of our fresh and sanitary bathroom. As I was doing so, and feeling particularly lighthearted, I heard a gurgling sound coming through the now-open window.

I had mistakenly thought it would be a problem for privacy if the window was open. By bending down, I could see the angle was such that you would need your face down at the pavement, to see in. And all this time, the fumes could have been drawn outdoors through the open window, instead of into our room.

Then it hit me. The gurgling sound was the water I had just released, and it emptied into the groove. I ran to the vestibule, put on my shoes, and looked.

We thought we had been using a urinal. Instead, we had been using the handwashing basin. It had been trickling outside, into the groove surrounding the base of the row house.

My inability to read cultural cues had made me a disgusting oaf. I saw myself through Japanese eyes, and I didn't like the barbarian I saw.

I vowed to be more careful and never to make assumptions again. There wasn't right or wrong, just different, and I was determined to learn those differences as quickly as possible.

This difficult and unpleasant experience changed everything. It forced me to communicate in Japanese. It allowed me to emerge with an unaccustomed social confidence. From that time forward, I was able to take control of situations as never before. I had turned a corner.

A week passed, and finally, my urgent visits to the bank paid off. After reimbursing my roommate, I went to the used-bicycle store, where I said goodbye to Minky MoMo.

I gradually awoke to how insufficient my completely Western education had been. There was so much we Westerners had yet to learn from Japan and the East. My curiosity about Japanese history and culture grew as my Japanese improved.

DO DO THAT VOODOO
THAT YOU DO SO WELL

I n 1985, the U.S. government recruited Americans who could speak Japanese to work at the Tsukuba Expo.[13] That meant that, this time, I would be considerably closer to Tokyo!

The Tsukuba Expo is where I fell in love—deeply and irredeemably in love. I went often to visit her where she hung out and to stroke her hair, that long black hair. The clerks at the shop watched me, but I didn't care. I was in love. I knew she could change my life forever.

I visited her during my lunch breaks in front of the stationary

---

13   The Tsukuba Expo was a fantasyland of technological advancements featuring laser lights, robots, and artificial intelligence. At my international village dorm room, we could plug an almost infinite number of electrical cords into two parallel grooves in the baseboard, along the entire perimeter. We were early guinea pigs for the washing toilets Japan is now famous for. After making use of the toilet in a standing position, many a gentleman pushed the wrong one of many buttons and received a face wash instead. We learned also to tape a bottle cap over the button that summoned the emergency medical technicians.

shop, her hair hanging down. I couldn't stop thinking about her. How good we could be together!

I always passed by the Korean pavilion on my way home, just to get another look. But by that time, they had usually taken her inside.

Days passed, and I began to have proprietary feelings toward her. I worried that someone else may also fall victim to her charms. Would they steal her away from me?

I knew it was unseemly out in the open, but I held her just to imagine how it might be. She was heavy and looked it. At six feet tall, she was bigger than any brush I had ever used before. Her ferrule was as big as my head. The expo would be over in a week.

The clerk in the stationer's shop was expecting me. "You want to know about the brush, of course. It's our signboard, so we can't let go of it just yet. When people see it, they want to come in."

They showed me their slate inkstones, ink sticks, paper, and little brushes—inconsequential sisters of my most imposing brush, which I was told had been made from the tails of 30 horses.

"We weren't thinking of selling it," he said. "It isn't really merchandise. But we didn't sell as many inkstones as we had hoped, so we'll have to consolidate freight for the shipping home. I'll see what we can do for you. Do you mind coming back tomorrow? I'll give you an answer then."

Before leaving, I straightened the tangles passersby had made in her hair.

I couldn't sleep that night. I wanted her to be the brush she was meant to be—not merely a pretty showstopper for a stationer's shop. And I could at last create the paintings I had dreamed of. We were meant for each other!

The next morning, I was at the shop before it opened, and I got my answer. It was yes! The cost was a stretch but less than I had feared.

In just a few weeks, my family met my plane back in the States and wondered at my silly grin. I had sent my other belongings straight to school in Pittsburgh, but I kept the brush with me.

A brush? What was all this excitement over a brush? The minute we arrived home, I undid the silk wrappings.

Wow! Words were not necessary. Her allure was obvious.

In just a few days, the time came to return to Carnegie Mellon for the school year. It was so difficult to leave Japan. I'd been fortunate enough to find the pigments I needed, but unable to buy them, I was no closer to being able to paint with them. I knew that I would have to continue my pursuit of those pigments when it was next possible.

At the bus station, I searched until I found the driver who was going to Pittsburgh.

As I approached the bus, the locks of *her* hair spilled out of the silk wrappings. The driver had seen my brush. His eyes popped open at the sight.

He said, "Don't you bring that voodoo thing on *my* bus!"

I had to take her completely out to prove she was a giant brush. "See? It's a tool of my trade," I said. "I'm a painter, and it's only a brush."

After I had belittled her so, I felt she deserved a heartfelt apology—something like *Please forgive me, o voluminous beauty!* But I restrained myself.

The driver shook his head. "Well, okay. But don't you be doin' no voodoo on *my* bus!"

I Know You Can

O n my return to Carnegie Mellon, I had a renewed relish for painting. And with that came confidence. My experience in Japan showed me that the constricting edicts of a few galleries in New York were not all there was to the world, not even the art world. I was determined to paint as I felt inspired even if I risked being kicked out.

Though what I saw as the bankrupt attitudes of modernism were still in full force, they no longer had sway over me. My paintings acted as an aesthetic reaction to the austerity of modernism. I returned to painting the beauty of flowers and trees, aware that beauty was considered weak and merely decorative. But this new confidence of mine became persuasive. This unapologetic use of beauty became a revolutionary act.

By the end of senior year, my paintings were strong and complex enough to exceed decorativeness. And I met with an approval I was not expecting. As an art major at Carnegie Mellon University, my graduation required that I hold a senior exhibition of my work. I put everything into that exhibition.

So in that final week, one of the last things I did was to exhibit at Forbes, a gallery on the edge of campus. I waited to see if anyone would come. To my surprise, one of my childhood heroes walked through the door.

As a child, I had often watched a television show called *Mister Rogers' Neighborhood*. In his daily show, Fred Rogers gave kindly, respectful encouragement to young children and addressed important issues they faced.

In our teen years, my sister and I thought we had outgrown his program. When wishing each other well with an exam or other daunting challenge, we might mimic Mr. Rogers and say, "You can do it. I know you can!"

I was in the back room of the gallery talking with some friends when I heard a familiar voice I couldn't quite place.

"Would it be possible to speak with the artist?"

I didn't want to miss greeting a patron, and I stepped out to the great surprise of seeing Mr. Rogers standing in the middle of the gallery. His recording studio was next to the campus.

He'd liked what he had seen in the windows and wanted to see more of the art on display.

I allowed him time to look. After I gathered the courage to approach him, he asked me to introduce him to the artist. I smiled and told him that would be me. He expressed surprise that I was not what he expected. He thought the artist would be an elderly Japanese woman.

I asked him why he thought that, and he said the level of accomplishment led him to believe the artist was older; the themes were Japanese; and he sensed a woman's sensitivity and introspection.

I was none of those things—but I told him my dream of becoming a professional artist.

"You can do it, Allan. I mean it. You can succeed," he said. "I know you'll go far!"

I was so excited I could hardly wait to get back to my apartment and call home.

"You remember how he would tell his TV audience 'You can do it!' Well, he liked my paintings so much he said it right to my face!"

The funny thing is, though Dad hadn't asked, I can remember even now what I was wearing that day.

I don't make light of Mr. Rogers anymore.

SILKEN THREADS

I n my last week at Carnegie Mellon, we went to the Carnegie Museum of Art on the invitation of my professor, Sam Gilliam. Like a coach, Professor Gilliam gathered us before my favorite Jackson Pollock painting.

He asked me to come up and lie down on the floor, look up at the painting, and describe what I saw. "Do you feel it? That's powerful stuff."

It was as if the painting washed over me like a wave. The same kind of energy we sense in nature was in that painting. I saw it animated, as flecks and dribs moved in my periphery.

He addressed the class. "You know the only difference between your paintings and this?" He said, "*This* one's in the museum."

That was the ultimate pep talk. Soon we would be like baby spiders catching currents of air with our silken threads.

Some graduates returned to their hometowns. Others flew off to New York. My silken thread was to take me back to Japan and this time for good. It would change my life forever. I was going to try to study at graduate school in Japan, hopefully under a decorated master. I couldn't see any other way to get access to the mineral pigments I needed.

After my senior exhibit, it was time to pack up all my supplies and clean out my studio space. As I was boxing up the last of my things, Professor Olds came out of his studio. I apologized for being under his nose for the last few years.

He said, "Well, I'll miss you. I've enjoyed watching your art develop over time. Remind me which school you came from. You transferred here sophomore year, right?"

"Uh ... no, I started here freshman year. Actually, I was in your class, but I took a few years off to live in Japan before I returned."

He was clearly surprised. "So, you're the one who left after freshman year?" After an awkward pause, he said, "You look so different, I didn't make the connection. That trip to Japan gave you focus. It had the right effect. So, what are your plans now?"

"As soon as I get enough money together, I'm going back to Japan. I'm going to try to get into a master's program there, but I'm not sure how realistic that is."

"Excellent," he said. "I can see why."

So, Professor Olds held no grudge after all. Moreover, he gave his blessings to my plan of returning to Japan. With that and Mr. Rogers's encouragement, I left for my parents' home in Washington, DC, to prepare for the move. After my first experiences in Japan, I knew how to live economically. I just needed enough money to live on until

I could settle into life in the world's costliest city, Tokyo.

―――――――――

A Washington attorney and art collector, Daniel Q. Callister, and his wife, Jan, had seen my works on the walls of my parents' home. When they commissioned a large mural for their entrance hall, I suddenly knew the possibility of going to Japan was opened to me.

VOUCHING FOR THE BARBARIAN

Upon completing the commission for the Callisters that* summer, I was able to pay for the trip to Japan. The timing
couldn't have been better. I sat on the plane, contemplat-
ing the full meaning of the decision to make Tokyo my home.

From my previous experience there, I knew I would have to brace
myself for three predictable challenges.

First, I would need to make peace with being treated as an
outsider and accept that as a condition of my choice. I would always
be a foreigner. But I decided I must not let that bother me if I was to
make Japan my home.

Second, at the emperor's advanced age, I suspected he would
"disintegrate honorably," as the Japanese say. Words directly associated with death are not used for the emperor. As he was the last
emperor to be considered a god, I suspected there would be a cultural

upheaval with that event. There wasn't. The same system of democratic monarchy continued.

The third was a much more worrisome issue: *the big one.* A cataclysmic earthquake was overdue, after having hit Tokyo historically at regular 80-year intervals. Every few years, a series of temblors would keep us on our toes, and panicky tabloid headlines served as a reminder whenever their sales flagged. Earthquakes, along with volcanoes, typhoons, conflagrations, and tsunamis, have all influenced the culture, societal fabric, and emotional makeup of Japan and its people.

When I had been at Carnegie Mellon, my friend Sach Takayasu shared some Japanese magazines with me. In reading them, I made a discovery. Few art supply stores in Japan sold the kind of pigment I needed. Fortunately, a couple of them were near Tokyo University of the Arts.

This time I was going to Tokyo.

When I first arrived, the uppermost thing on my mind was preparing for the entrance exams at that university. But first I would need to find permanent housing.

I started out at youth hostels. The rules dictated that I could stay only three days at a time, so I had to alternate between two places, one of which had been a dormitory for the 1964 Olympics. I hoped to find a place within a mile of the university, but my search had its challenges. Without even checking, most real estate agents simply said they had nothing for me. More often, they would purposely ignore me.

One day I was looking in the show window of the Akamon Real Estate office in Hongo. Long strips of paper said To Rent or To Sell at the top in red letters. They listed prices and square footage according to how many standard-sized tatami mats would fit in the space. A tatami mat is a thick floor covering made of rushes. Roughly three-feet-by-six-feet, it is approximately the size of the average person lying down with arms crossed.

After looking at the paper strips, I worked up my courage to step inside and ask about two of the more reasonable rooms I saw advertised. But before I did, one of the agents rushed out to meet me.

"Shoo! Skat! Go away!"

At first, I turned around expecting to see a dog. I didn't realize he was talking to me.

"Get away from here! I can't have you around. What would my people think if they saw you here? Go!"

I was so upset at his reaction to me as a foreigner that I had to go back to the youth hostel and calm down. The next morning it took more than the usual courage to resume my search.

Days passed before I found an agent in Nezu who was willing to help me. After not even being allowed to look at a room, I was willing to accept almost anything.

The man searched his files and said, "Here's one without windows." As a consolation, he added, "But it comes with furniture." We went to see it.

The place was pitch black. I heard a shuffling sound as I stepped in, and a sour stench hit my nose. He fumbled for the pull cord, and a blue-green florescent light blinked on. Countless black cockroaches and gray rats scrabbled for cover under a pile of stained bedding. Scattered plates from months-old, half-eaten meals littered the mushy tatami mats. I tried to hold down my lunch as I ran out.

—————

Days later, while continuing to search for a room, my spirits low, I heard a voice behind me. "Aren't you Allan?"

Sometimes being a foreigner and standing out in a crowd has its advantages. What incredible luck! It was Mr. Shibuya. Shibuya-san. We had met through the close-knit community of Japanese people living in Pittsburgh. He had an empty shed in his garden and was kind enough to let me stay there while I continued my search. I didn't have to feel quite so harried. After moving in and transporting my luggage, I crossed the street and relaxed in the public bath.

Mr. Shibuya introduced me to Hayashi-san, a nervous young man about my age. As the assistant to a local real estate agent, Hayashi-san was well-enough acquainted with the neighborhood to know of a closet that might be available, and he would take me to see it. The place was only four tatami mats—under a staircase.

Stepping stones led to a gate between yellow *yamabuki* bushes. *Fatsia* and *nanten* blossomed on either side of the entrance to a late-19th-century rooming house. It had been built for students of Tokyo University when it was still called the Imperial University.

We put our shoes in the chest and walked past the shared kitchen to the end of the polished wooden hallway. Over a long copper-lined sink, mirrors were surrounded by sunny windowpanes. I would need to use the neighborhood public bath.

The room was cramped, allowing only enough space for a low table or a futon, but not both at once. A triangular closet under the stairs had barely space for storing one or the other. My heart was in the moss garden out the window, which added character to the place. "I'll take it," I said.

We went out to the house of the landlord. Hayashi-san stayed in the vestibule mopping his brow with a handkerchief. Old man Tsukioka appeared in his long drawers and a knit waist warmer. He asked Hayashi, "Does he have a guarantor?"

Hayashi said, "Yes, I'll vouch for him."

Old Tsukioka-san stared at him as if to say *You must be joking!* He then ushered me into a room just big enough to hold the two of us. Tracing lines in the ash of the hibachi that separated us, he asked if I liked listening to vaudeville storytellers.

"Yes, I do. Very much."

Apparently, that was a test, and I had passed. He handed me the skeleton key.

Finally, I had my feet on the ground—Tokyo ground. I could prepare for the entrance exam. I would paint with a fury and work on my reading and writing.

I went back to Shibuya-san to thank him for the use of the shed, gave him the good news, and got my belongings together. Not 20 minutes later, I went across the way for a final bath. Over the dividing wall, I could hear women gossiping.

"Did you hear? You know the foreigner? Yes, at the Shibuyas'. He's going to move."

From that day on, at least once a month, Hayashi would, in clever and subtle ways, come to check up on me—his new liability.

Hayashi-san was also instrumental in finding my first Tokyo studio. It was small. I had to turn the tatami mats wrong side up and paint on plastic sheeting. The owner planned to tear the place down as soon as the other contracts expired.

The key didn't work properly in the lock, but a deftly wielded palette knife could open the door. Yet with all its drawbacks, nothing could dampen my affection for the place.

TABLOID CLASSROOM

I *couldn't paint until I found a pigment store* that would sell to me. I soon discovered one near the university. Sugita-san, the owner of Kinkaido, was open, friendly, and always happy to answer my questions. She was the first friend I made in Tokyo. She was surprised that I knew so much about the technique even though I had no formal training. Sugita-san was patient in giving me ad hoc hints and technical tips, and hers were the first instructions in nihonga I had in Japan.

Another pressing issue was that I would need to hurry and get (and maintain) a visa. Luckily, I was fluent in conversational Japanese by this time. However, for the entrance exam, I would need to master reading and writing—and fast.

In the early 1980s, language-acquisition texts were usually written for children. I found the most helpful substitutes for Japanese language texts were the tabloids. The writing was in colloquial Japanese and simple enough that I could figure out the general meaning. With titles like *Focus*, or *Flash*, they evoked nosy photojournalism.

I preferred *Focus*. On the right-hand page, they placed a full-page photograph, and on the left was a description of the picture in colloquial Japanese. I spent valuable study time at the magazine rack of the corner store. I needed every spare yen for art supplies, but I was not the only one who couldn't afford to buy them. At any one time, two or three of us could be found there.

Every so often, the owner would come over with a sigh of exasperation and dust or rearrange the magazines, but we returned like flies. Maybe I should have been embarrassed at reading such "trash," but it was an effective way to study the complex kanji characters.

TRUTH AND BEAUTY

A *group of friends got together who were related* to my earlier stint teaching English. On the way home, about eight of us were walking to the train station. I tend to walk rather fast and had to make myself slow down to stay with the group.

One time, as I found myself ahead of the group, I noticed a woman with long straight hair down to her waist out in front of me. She was about my age, dressed well, and walked with confidence. I caught up with her and introduced myself.

"I see you walk fast too." That was probably the stupidest opening line ever. But she seemed to be flattered and asked me what I was doing in Japan. I knew she would assume I taught English as did most of the group.

I had only recently rented the studio across the moss garden from my room; instead of telling her I was temporarily making a living teaching English, I could tell her what I actually was.

"I'm an artist. Well ... I mean a nihonga painter."

That took her by surprise. To the Japanese, the possibility of becoming a nihonga painter was closed to anyone who was not born to it.

"Really? I'd like to see what you do."

"Sure! I mean absolutely! Yes, that would be great."

"I'm Mami." She explained her name was written with the kanji that stood for *truth and beauty.*

"I'm Allan. I'm told my name means *harmony* in the Celtic language."

I had only recently gotten a phone, and I had to look for my number. It felt pushy to give her my number, but not as creepy as it would have been to ask for hers. My hope was that she would be interested enough to give me a call. After we separated, I regretted not asking for her phone number anyway.

I sent an aerogram home, saying I had met a remarkable woman who was very nice.

I was painting in my studio when I heard the phone ring below in my room across the garden. There was no way I could rush out, go down the steps, pass the three houses, go out by the street through the gate, get around the back of the boardinghouse, unlock my door, and pick up the phone before the caller would hang up.

The caller was far more likely to be that remarkable woman than a gallery owner. This happened several times, to my absolute frustration. I investigated the possibility of getting another phone but instead got a phone jack with two outlets.

I bought a long telephone cord and, secretly, one day climbed out my studio window, down onto the rock wall that separated my studio from my room. I had to be extra sneaky, as it was over the moss garden behind my landlord's home. I hid the cord in the ivy lining the wall then tossed the rest of the cord into the half-opened window. A ninja's outfit seemed appropriate for the job.

After getting the second phone hooked up, it took a week before the phone rang again. To my great relief, it was Mami.

She had an errand that would take her through my side of the city. If I was free tomorrow night, would I be interested in meeting? I was!

It took most of that night and the next day just to arrange my paintings and make my studio acceptable, if not presentable. I was to wait for her call.

She called later than I had expected. She was waiting for me in a coffee shop, so I got my bicycle out and rushed off. It took a while to find what looked like the place. But when I stepped in, I couldn't see her anywhere. Perhaps it was the wrong shop. I was about to leave when she stood up and waved. She was sitting in the very back obscured by a fern divider.

She was more beautiful than I had remembered.

She told me about her trip to the States and asked some questions about English that she couldn't answer for her students.

I really liked her. But I had never felt more like a foreigner, and that feeling stung. She had called me to help her with her work, not because she might have feelings for me beyond that. I was no more than a convenient dispenser of English knowledge.

She didn't seem to have any interest in asking about my painting or any such thing. Though I had spoken Japanese the whole time during that first meeting, she only spoke English with me at the coffee shop.

I sent an aerogram home: "Never mind. She's just an English bandit."

LOVE. SICK.

A *month passed. The same group decided to take* a day trip to the scenic mountains of Nagatoro. A friend had rented a van, and early one autumn morning, we all piled in. I am not a great car passenger, and as a child, I frequently got motion sickness. What was worse, as the last person to be picked up, I sat in the foldout seat in the very back.

From the foot of the crimson mountains, we gradually ascended by a series of increasingly short hairpin turns and switchbacks. It was like being tossed on the ocean by a hurricane, and the others in the group were enjoying it. I tried yawning and popping my ears. I tried keeping my eyes closed, but nothing helped. I feared I wasn't going to make it. It was too late to ask them to stop because I no longer dared open my mouth to make that request.

In answer to my most fervent prayers, the van ground to a stop in the gravel parking lot at the top of the mountain.

I stumbled to a building that had a lobby with a sofa and lay down with my eyes closed. Even closed, my eyes were spinning. My breathing had to take my nausea into account, which caused puffing and groaning noises.

Soon I heard similar sounds from an abutting sofa. It seemed I was not the only passenger who was miserably carsick. Neither of us had noticed the scenery along the way. We both expressed amazement and relief at making it this far without major embarrassment.

After a time, nausea no longer dominated our conversation, and we turned to the subject of classical music—favorite composers, art, and favorite artists. Not only was it a great distraction from the churning, but I was also surprised at how similar our taste in art, music, and literature was.

This gradually deepening familiarity was new and intoxicating to me, and I didn't want it to end. But all too soon, it was night, and our adventurous friends returned. Gathering around us, they were surprised we hadn't moved in all that time.

"You missed some incredible scenery. Well, at least you're not moaning anymore. Will you two be able to make it down the mountain okay?"

As we went to the van, I got my first good look.

It was Mami!

We sat next to each other in the front seat on the way back, and I realized why I hadn't recognized her. She had braided her long straight black hair the night before, and when she undid it that morning, it created a mass of wild hair that covered her shoulders and flew around her face in crimped skeins.

This was a most unexpected and welcome surprise. That first meeting in the coffee shop had been a failure. We had both been unnaturally formal and nervous. This was the essential redo that the fates had found necessary. It had taken carsickness to break the ice—to let us be real instead of trying to meet assumed expectations.

At the end of the trip, I made a point of getting her number. And I sent home an aerogram saying, "She's wonderful."

When I spoke with Mami on the phone, I said I would love to see her again on the condition that we only speak Japanese. I told her why, and she understood.

But she brought up a condition of her own: she had to see my artwork. She wasn't sure she could like an artist if she didn't like his art.

A letter arrived from home: "So, you met another girl?"

As the day of her visit arrived, I was concerned. Though we did like many of the same artists, I painted like none of them. There was a real possibility that she wouldn't like my paintings. First, she never mentioned any nihonga artists. Her favorites had all been Western oil painters. Second, she was quite particular about her preferences, which was a good thing. But they were all famous painters who had painted in their prime. I was just 25.

It was essential for this to go well.

I led her up the stone steps to my studio and pulled the door open. She stepped inside and looked silently at the creative disorder. I let her take her time. She pointed to the panel of wisteria among colorful swirls, against a deep green background.

She moved it into the light of the window. "My family name, Ito, is written with the character for wisteria."

The panel had been in front of another painting of wisteria floating amid golden clouds before a royal-blue sky. "This ... this is the color I see when I dream of heaven."

There was a long, satisfied pause.

"I hope you will always paint heaven," she said.

I sent an aerogram home: "It's the same girl, and she's not an English bandit."

On occasion I would find some freshly cooked spaghetti had been quietly set out by the studio door with an encouraging note: "This is to help you work. I didn't want to disturb you—Your devotee."

25

DAIKU

Mami and I spent a lot of time together on weekends and often as much as three hours talking on the phone each night.

On one such call, she mentioned how much she loved *Daiku*.

I panicked. Daiku? What or who was *Daiku*?

She said she couldn't love someone who didn't genuinely appreciate Daiku.

Oh no! I'd have to figure out what it was. And fast.

She said she had broken up with a guy once because he didn't even know what Daiku was!

Daiku? Daiku! What could this be? Too much was riding on this. I mustn't get it wrong! Hmm ... *dai* could signify a sequence of numbers. Or maybe *platform*? What about *ku*? That could be just about anything!

My mind was racing. I couldn't let this go much longer without responding, so I said with desperation, "Oh, I *absolutely* appreciate Daiku!"

Mami said she was extremely relieved. She then asked what part of Daiku I liked best.

Uh-oh, I had really done it! I had dug myself into a hole. So, it was something with parts? That could help.

She kept talking. Meanwhile, I tried to pay attention and at the same time solve this conundrum: *Ku* could be a district. It could be pain. No, that wouldn't make sense. Could it be a phrase, like in a poem or a piece of music? Oh! It could mean to fabricate, like in carpenter, because the symbol for carpenter is formed with both big and fabricate. Yes, that must be it!

Just in time, she exclaimed, "Can you believe it? He thought Daiku was a carpenter!" She clearly thought her former friend had demonstrated a lack of culture.

Whew, what a relief that I hadn't blurted out *carpenter*!

Ku could also be the number nine. *Dai* and *ku* could signify the ninth something. Or was it the ninth of something?

She continued by declaring she always felt elevated after Daiku.

I thought I had it! Oh, please let this be right! I was guessing it was Beethoven's Ninth Symphony, and I was ready to go out on a limb.

I said I thought even though many people prefer Beethoven's Fifth or his *Eroica*, I had to agree nothing elevated like his Ninth.

I started to hum it. I figured, if I had to go down, it might as well be in flames.

She proclaimed she couldn't start the year without it.

Wait, what? I thought I had blown it! What I had just said must not have made sense.

I had run out of options. It was time to confess I had no idea what I was talking about.

She must have sensed my confusion, because she wondered if Americans didn't celebrate the New Year by listening to Beethoven's Ninth, like the Japanese.

Sweet confirmation! Oh, how close I had come to the precipice. I danced a triumphant jig, jerking the phone off the table with a crash. "*Freude! Freude!* All creatures drink of joy. This kiss is for all the world!"[14]

When I caught my breath, I replied, "In America, we usually listen to Handel's *Messiah*."

"Oh, I've sung in the *Messiah* before and the Daiku as well," she said. "But are you okay, Allan? You sound winded."

"No, I'm fine."

I was very fine.

"Whoever has created an abiding friendship or has won a true and loving wife ... join our song of praise!" These words of the chorus have taken on special significance.

---

14 This is my favorite English translation of the poem by Johann Christoph Friedrich von Schiller, "Ode to Joy" 1785. It was the inspiration by which Ludwig van Beethoven wrote his ninth symphony, and serves as the lyrics for the chorus. Translator unknown.

FIG LEAF, PLEASE!

Mami and I had dated for about two years when it came time to meet her parents. Mr. Ito sent an itinerary in his bold, precise calligraphic writing. We were to meet at Morioka, halfway between their home and Tokyo. The train we were to take had been carefully decided, and we were to meet at the hotel near the station. I knew Mr. Ito was a school principal who liked to plan things out carefully. That was all I had heard.

On the bullet train hurtling out of Tokyo, I felt like a nervous wreck, but Mami held my hand. She was my best ally.

My apprehension sent me to the restroom. Passing the mirror, I saw my hair was a mess and my shirt was buttoned all wrong. Why did I have to look so ... foreign?

I hadn't known what to wear. I realized my dad probably wouldn't have approved, so very likely Mami's wouldn't either. She told me whatever I wore would be fine. It didn't matter, because whatever it was, she always liked it. When I asked if my hair was all right, she said it looked great.

This was the first time I realized Mami was unable to be objective. It didn't matter how bad I looked—to her I always looked great. That was nice, but when I really needed feedback, she couldn't help. I fixed the buttons and wished I had made a special trip to the barber.

Mami was wearing a peacock-green dress. I was in a blue button-down oxford shirt and beige corduroys. At the knee, there was a paint stain I had tried unsuccessfully to remove.

When we met the Itos, Mami's father was in a navy suit and tie, and his wife wore a print dress. They took us to the restaurant and ordered for the table. As I am left-handed, I sat across from her parents and to the left of Mami, where we were able to hold hands under the table.

Mr. Ito's face was wreathed in genuine smiles, and he seemed pleased when the meal came—the food was delicious.

We made small talk. How was the ride up? Were we concerned by the recent surge of seismic activity in Tokyo? Mrs. Ito spoke quietly, with her head tilted to one side, eager to hear the answer. There was a musical tone to her voice, and she spoke with a dignified grace and calmness.

I enjoyed getting to know them both over dinner, which made the experience more relaxed. The meal was a success and surprisingly stress-free.

After dinner, Mrs. Ito lightly touched the flowers in the lobby and identified each one.

"Well, time for a bath," Mr. Ito announced. "This is a famous hot spring here. Everything is already supplied. Shall we go up to change?"

Without the slightest emotional preparation, I watched Mami and her mother disappear into their room. Mr. Ito and I went into ours, where we changed into the *yukata* bathing kimono provided by the hotel. Hoping to score points, I tied the sash properly, with care. We picked up our towels and headed for the hot spring.

I expected to see Mami and her mother again by the entrance before going into the women's side, but they were taking their time. I would not see them until the next morning. Were they talking about me?

Without a comforting glance from Mami, my only ally, Mr. Ito and I plunged through the slotted curtains at the entrance of the changing room. Within two hours of meeting my girlfriend's father, I was fumbling with the tie on my kimono, preparing to appear completely naked in front of him.

I had become accustomed to the public baths by then. But until this moment, everyone else there had been disinterested and anonymous. I was conscious of being given a serious once-over. But, as we began washing up, the conversation became pleasant and focused mostly on the meal we had just enjoyed. I could hear Mami's voice from the women's side.

Soon the bath was over. Warm and relaxed, we were ready for sleep. As I slipped into my soft futon, Mr. Ito turned off the lights.

Before I could fall asleep, he asked, "How serious are you about my daughter?"

"I am very serious."

I hadn't expected to ask for his daughter's hand in marriage here and now! My mind raced as I tried to sort out what Japan's equivalent of Emily Post might say was the proper procedure.

Do I propose first and then speak with her parents? Or should I check with them first before it is time to propose?

"Yes, I am serious about Mami. I have been considering proposing to her, but I've been trying to find the right time."

He said, "I have a few thoughts about the timing." That sounded helpful. "What are your plans for the future?"

"Well, I plan on making my living as a painter. A nihonga artist painter."

"I see. I hear that's a very difficult profession to make a good living. And forgive me for being blunt, but do you think anyone would buy nihonga by a foreigner? And a complete unknown? To be honest, I wonder if you can expect a proper income to support a family. You'll want children, of course."

I was faced with the harsh truth. And I could see it from his perspective only too well. I had vowed to accept whatever privations a career in art would bring but assumed I would be facing those trials alone. That was before I met Mami.

What was I thinking? She had called herself my devotee. I wouldn't want to cause her the least difficulty, but here I was making unrealistic assumptions.

"Well, I'm applying to Tokyo University of the Arts. My expectation, uh, my hope, is that a diploma from there would provide me with the validation I would need to build a career in art in Japan."

"I see. That seems a bit overconfident. This is the most difficult program in Asia. You know that only one in every fifty applicants is accepted? And that is Japanese applicants. I've never even heard of a Westerner being accepted to such a school. Isn't that right?"

"Uh ... yes, sir, I think that's probably right."

"I'm sure you realize I would need some kind of assurance that you have a future. I have only one daughter. I think you see my point."

"Yes, sir. I do."

He was courteous but firm as he continued. "I wouldn't like the thought of her living overseas. You aren't planning on taking her abroad, are you?"

"No. Even if I wanted to, that wouldn't be possible. The materials for making nihonga can't be purchased abroad."

"I see." There was a long pause, and he began again. "I'd like to suggest a condition to my approval."

I was fully awake. I understood this was how a loving father must look out for his daughter. The dinner in my stomach shifted as I listened.

"I'm not a good judge of art and have no way of predicting your prospects as an artist. I'll have to leave it to the judgment of the professors of the Tokyo University of the Arts. If you are admitted, I will approve. Will you accept those conditions?"

That was a sobering thought. I didn't like the odds and being without a backup plan. Until now, I had thought my relationship with Mami was fated—inevitable. I would need to show my confidence and get him used to the idea of my being tied to Mami's future.

My voice cracked as I said, "Yes, I will."

"Will you give up on the idea of marrying Mami if you don't get in?"

He just sealed the final loophole. I *must* be accepted into the university for all aspects of my future—*our* future. Every emotion rebelled against my agreeing to his terms, and yet I could see no way around it.

"Yes," I said. "I want Mami to be happy. And if her ... that is, if our relationship with you is strained, she wouldn't be happy. I accept the condition."

"That is a good answer. Well, good night, Allan." Mr. Ito rolled over.

All hope of sleep was destroyed, and I stared at the darkness where the ceiling should be. As the night wore on, I regretted the agreement.

I wanted to learn at the university, but I knew that it was a long shot. My plan had been that if I didn't get in, I could always figure out something else. What a fool I had been, with no idea what I was in for. It reminded me of the deal I made with my father. But in applying to Carnegie Mellon, at least, I had a shared language and cultural background. An American university allowed me to compete on my home court. Everything about this new challenge was going to be unfamiliar.

On the train going home, I was more than usually quiet. Mami asked what was on my mind. It was the agreement I had made with her father at the hot springs of Morioka, and I told her so.

"After losing both his father and stepfather to the war," she said, "my father had an uncertain upbringing. He chose to become a public servant so his livelihood would be assured. He just wants the same security for me as he has created for himself." She understood how strongly these experiences influenced his strict requirements. She knew as I did that he had carefully thought this out. It was not up for debate.

I regretted putting our relationship at risk, but he hadn't given me any choice. It would have meant giving up Mami—something I was not willing to do.

The stakes were a lot higher now, and I was playing an away game.

Much of the time that followed was controlled by my work and completely focused on painting. From then on, we worked as a team. As Mami and I kept our eyes on the future, some of our telephone calls had to decrease in length.

There were, however, some wonderful time-savers that she provided—especially the many delicious hot meals Mami frequently left at my studio door.

PLAYING AN AWAY GAME

I *often relive the first day of the exam* at Tokyo University of the Arts.

About 30 of us were placed in each empty classroom to wait. Staring at the walls, I tried to slow my breathing. The stale odor of smoke made me nauseous. Was it from centuries of tobacco? Maybe it was from the kerosene stoves in the winter and mosquito coils in summer.

We were finally ushered into an exam room lined with benches known as *horses*. The neck of each horse supported a sheet of drawing paper taped on a board. After locating my assigned number on one of the papers, I straddled my horse.

In the center was a chair on a raised platform. A nude model entered and sat on it. This was just a normal pose, I thought—nothing especially difficult. I expected the more complicated poses would come later. We were to use pencils for the entrance exam, in the European tradition. No ink, no brushes.

The schedule on the wall indicated we would have 20 minutes for drawing, then a ten-minute rest. We'd alternate this way for seven hours, with a one-hour break for lunch. At a signal, we were permitted to touch the paper.

Twenty minutes. The same length of time we had per pose at Carnegie Mellon.

Ever conscious of the clock, I mustn't hurry and make a mistake or leave anything undone. Just as I was finishing, the proctor called, "Stop!" He ushered us out, and all the assistants walked in.

Why did our 10-minute break seem so long? I guessed it took awhile to gather our papers and give us new ones. I wondered what the next pose would be.

As we were taken back into the room, I was puzzled. My drawing was still there.

Why? How could I get a blank sheet? At first glance, the others appeared to have received blank papers. Cautiously, I looked more closely.

No, most of them had a few tentative marks on them.

During the next break, we assumed talking was forbidden. However, a comradeship of the trenches made us open up, and we talked in hushed tones.

Are we supposed to do the same pose all day? I asked. The answer was yes.

In the next 10-minute break, I wondered why everyone was drawing the feet so big.

The answer was not reassuring: "Because my teacher in cram

school said the professors like it that way. Something about the feet looking like they're attached to the soil."

We went back to the room. I looked at my drawing and saw that I'd committed myself to normal-sized feet. If I tried to make them larger, they would extend off the edge. My stomach churned.

How many more hours were left? I'd have to focus on details and highlights. I didn't think I could keep this up.

28

BOW, SIT, WAIT

T he second day of the exam took the form of an interview. I was to defend the two paintings I had submitted. As we all waited in turn, I observed the formal way the others opened the door, bowed before crossing the threshold, and closed the door.

A new comrade-in-the-trenches told me there was a proper way to walk into the room. Arms at your side, bow. Cross the room to the chair. Sit, hands folded in lap. Bow again and wait to be addressed.

When my turn came, my paintings were already on easels. All the professors of the nihonga department—three of the Five Mountains of Nihonga—sat at a long table. I was in the middle of the room.

An assistant professor spoke first. "We don't know of a Mr. Sam Gilliam and cannot confirm that your translation of his letter of recommendation is accurate. Can you show us where he features in *Who's Who of American Art*?"

I had never heard of such a thing, but I said, "I will try."

Professor Kayama took over. He said he appreciated my enthusiasm for pioneering new subject matter for nihonga. "Why did you apply to study under me?"

I swallowed. "I've seen your students take individual approaches to expression. I believe that means you are the best person to guide me on my own path." To me, this was the sign of a truly great art teacher.

He said, "How did you know I would be teaching here? This is my first year. I've taught at Tama for the last thirty years."

He caught me off guard. "I just assumed you taught at your alma mater."

"I see. So, tell me about this painting."

It was a gnarled green pine tree. The background was red, sprinkled with square-cut gold leaf. I said, "My hope was that it wouldn't require an explanation."

"How did you get the paint so smooth? It is well done technically. But it isn't your *own* path, is it?"

His instruction had already begun. I didn't know what to say, so I bowed. That seemed the thing to do when nothing else came to mind.

He said, "OK. Thank you."

Was that my cue to go? Maybe I should have told him how I got the paint so smooth. Or was that a rhetorical question? It was too late now. I stood and bowed, feeling drained. It had not gone well.

"By the way," he said, "supposing you are not accepted into the program, would you be interested in auditing the course?"

"Yes, absolutely," I said. I wanted to learn. That was more important to me than a degree.

"All right then, thank you."

What was I to make of that? Was this good news—or a way to soften the blow of rejection?

Was this his way of keeping this barbarian docile or making me leave Japan?

———

A few grueling weeks later, the results were to be announced. I had the engagement ring in my pocket and was planning on going straight to Mami's apartment to propose the moment I learned I was accepted. The applicants all gathered outdoors in a drizzle, before a large plywood bulletin board. A scroll was rolled out and pinned to the board. Countless numbers fell in columns under different headings. As we searched for our numbers, squeals and exclamations of joy or disappointment broke out. Art history. Aesthetics. Restoration. Western art. Nihonga. Was my number there? I couldn't see it. I looked again.

No, it wasn't.

This was bad. They didn't want me. How could I break the news to Mami? I went to a nearby payphone and spent all the change in my pockets in a conversation with Mami. It was punctuated by long silences. The path forward had become impossible to see, but we were going to take that path together.

I stopped by the registrar's office on the way out and picked up the application for auditing.

The engagement ring remained in my pocket.

29

MYSTERIOUS FOOTPRINTS

My application to audit was accepted. *I was* allowed to participate fully on a provisional basis but without getting credit. They set me up in a storage room that was larger than any studio I was used to. It had a window looking out over a collection of plaster sculptures. Dust was everywhere.

On the doorpost was a wooden plaque with my name on it. I was instructed to keep the room locked at all times, and whenever I left, I was to turn the plaque around so they could tell I was gone.

I was pleased to be included in critiques at the end of the semester. I had to make an impression, so I went to the extra expense of painting in a folding-screen format. The paint was too fluid to use an easel or stand the screens up while I painted. And the screens were too big for the table. So, I laid them on the floor and used two-by-four planks over them as a bridge to reach the center areas.

The dust in the studio was relentless, but I needed to leave it on the floor. It served an important purpose. Sometimes unexpected footprints appeared in the dust, and I once noticed a handout had been moved from a stool in my absence.

The assistant came to me about an important matter: He needed me to sweep the floor. I used a coarse bamboo broom to move the dust—much as a monk rakes the gravel of his Zen garden into patterns. After that, the suspicious footprints were even easier to see.

One rainy day, I was studying the painting I planned to submit for review. It was the last day of critiques before summer. Using many green pigments, I had painted a liquid green background to evoke the feeling of the long rainy season. The addition of a few ferns transformed it. Would it be enough?

Something was still missing. I opened my umbrella and went outside to seek inspiration in the dampness of Ueno Park next door. Heavy drops fell from the boughs of trees overhead. Hearing the croak of a frog, I followed the voice until I discovered its owner. He was an obliging model, and when I completed a sketch of him, he hopped away. Rushing back to the studio, I quickly added him to the green background and fanned the painting dry before taking it to the critique.

When my turn came, Kayama sensei said, "Oh, you've added a frog. Hmm ... yes, that makes all the difference."

Now the cat was out of the bag; all this time, it had been Professor Kayama who had left all those footprints on the floor. He had been my secret visitor! I avoided showing my surprise.

30

GOING COLD TURKEY

I *was rootling through a junk shop and found* a postcard written in the 19th century, before pencils and fountain pens were available in Japan. The man who wrote it was unknown to me, but he had an extraordinary ability with a brush.

His calligraphy was normal for the time—formal but decorative beyond the mere function of communicating an idea. What impressed me most was the ink sketch at the bottom. I had worked on creating expressive lines to put life into the plants I was painting. His facility for expressing himself with a brush was astounding. The lines of this little brushed sketch had all the vitality and passion conveyed by the artist El Greco.

How could this person, who I assumed had no formal art training, be better with a brush than professional artists of today? Such effects were made possible only by the subtle nuances of touch. I connected this concept with the obsolete word *taction.*

A pencil or pen hits the paper with varying strength. But aside from the depth caused by pressure, the line isn't significantly changed.

With a brush, subtle differences in its contact with paper are enough to vary the thickness of the line. The purposeful adjustment of those differences gives the line expressive variety. A brush is flexible. There is little resistance from the paper. We have no inborn sensitivity to the bristles' delicate resistance, so I suspected it took a lifetime of training.

When only brushes were available to the Japanese, brushes became almost an extension of the body—just as chopsticks can feel like an extension of the thumb and forefinger.

A truism came to my mind: The ideal time to plant a tree is 20 years ago, and the second most ideal time is right now. I knew I must completely eliminate the pen and pencil from my life immediately! That was 30 years ago.

I was determined to make the brush a natural extension of my hand. To accomplish that, I began using a *yatate*, a small silver box that holds ink and usually a tube to hold a brush. My first five yatate were all the size of a matchbox and fit into the watch pocket of my pants[15].

Two-thirds of each box contains cat whiskers. They operate somewhat like a stamp pad, able to transfer ink to a brush when lightly touched. Yet they absorb the ink so it won't leak in spite of vigorous motion. The other third is an inset that contains a brush with a collapsible silver ferrule.

---

15 My friend Robert DeMaria has recently written the seminal reference on all things yatate. DeMaria, Robert. Yatate Artistry Craftsmanship Utility. San Francisco: Yatate Kokusai LLC, 2019.

These brushes make a satisfying clink when I flick them out. I use them so much that I have to replace the brushes once every few months. Even the silver boxes need to be replaced every few years. A corner might wear down and start leaking ink.

One night in a restaurant, I explained something to a collector by drawing on a napkin. Later that night, I realized that I had forgotten my yatate in the restaurant. I called and asked if they had found my small box containing ink and a brush. They said no. But I was sure I had left it there, so I called back. Did they find my *silver lighter*? Yes, and they would keep it for me.

Because I had renounced the use of other writing implements, I became comfortable with the brush. I learned to make the thinnest, most delicate lines to fill in my small pocket calendar and telephone directory. Class notes were quicker to write in Japanese when I used a brush. Alphabetic curves were more difficult.

Japan's written language was clearly created with, and for, the brush. When I used to address exhibition announcements with a pen, I needed to rest my hand at regular intervals. But I could address them with a brush well into the night, as long as I could stay awake.

Those little silver boxes are no longer made. I need to keep my eyes open for antique yatate that were made before pocketed clothing came to Japan. They were meant to be worn sandwiched under an *obi* sash.

I have a yatate with a small place for a signature seal and red ink, to go with it; another with a place for two brushes that differ in size. My favorite has two ink receptacles, and another has ruled lines along the brush's tube for measuring.

My need for these small portable ink-and-brush containers I

use for sketching will keep me searching. As repositories of cultural history, junk shops and antique stores hold a special fascination for me. Therefore, the continuing search for the yatate is no burden whatsoever.

THIS IS NEVER DONE

I *enjoyed classes, painting, and getting to know the* real students. I went on sketching tours to the coast. And during the school festival, I helped carry the float for the nihonga department in the parade through Ueno Park. Though my studio was separate from the other students, I had made some lasting friends.

One day, as the year was ending, Professor Kayama sat on the chair in my studio and reminisced about his wartime experiences. "I'm glad you speak Japanese," he said. "The only English I learned was to beg from the occupying forces. I can say, 'Give me gum,' or, 'Give me chocolate.'"

I had no idea how to respond. He must have noticed my discomfort, because he changed the subject.

"I was glad for the end of the war," he said. "I could finally listen to jazz again."

He was about to leave, but first he turned to face me. "Oh, one more thing," he said. "I hope you'll apply again for the master's program. The entrance exam is coming up soon. Think about what paintings to submit."

The door closed, and he was gone. Did this mean I had another chance? After having been rejected, I was just glad I could audit their classes.

Wow. Just wow.

I would have to hurry. None of the paintings I had been working on were the prescribed size for an application.

Since the advent of Western art influences in Japan, the shape of a painting had been standardized according to some European method. The size was supposedly related to the number of postcards it took to cover the area. We were to paint two #50 paintings. Oddly enough, the number of postcards it takes to cover a #50 panel is closer to 40.

Until then, I had painted folding screens or made my own panels in whatever shape I wanted. But this time, even nihonga paintings had to fit into the European numbering system. I would have to come up with two paintings quickly.

Assuming a soak would help me think, I went to the public bath. My friend Morita-san was there. He was an assistant at Musashino University of Art's department of Western painting and was a great source of advice. He had helped me translate Sam Gilliam's letter of recommendation, using the special, formalized wording the Japanese expect in this instance.

As we spoke, I looked down at my college ring. It had turned green. When I remarked on that, Morita-san said, "Tonight, they're using water to approximate the hot springs. The chemicals have tarnished the silver."

He told me the pharmacy sold water from the same hot springs—which gave me an idea. I didn't want Kayama sensei to see what I was doing before the interview. So, I was careful to do all my experiments at home.

First, I would need two folding screens according to the size of a #50 European panel. My mounter, Tajiri-san, said this was never done. Such a shape did not exist. I asked if he could make an exception. Finally, I persuaded him that this disrespectful thing I was asking would not reflect badly on him. If his fellow mounters said anything, he could just blame it on some silly foreigner, a barbarian trampling down rules and traditions.

I wanted a twofold screen. Tajiri-san sucked air in through his teeth—the polite way Japanese avoid saying a blunt *no*. I knew he was right; I couldn't have a dividing line in the middle of the painting. And four panels would make the sections so thin as to be absurd. I finally understood why Japanese paintings didn't fit the European dimensions. Such rectangular proportions make a typical Japanese composition difficult.

I would need two three-paneled screens.

"I can do it," he said, "but a *byobu*[16] like this is going to need protection."

They would need boxes. Folding-screen panels are only made in even numbers so that when they close, it is like the covers of a book protecting the pages. An odd number means that one side remains exposed.

---

16 *Byobu* is the Japanese word for folding-screen painting.

After months of stinky and dangerous alchemical experimentation, my paintings were in their cedar boxes, delivered, and ready to be judged.

The figure-drawing exam ended without incident.

On the day of the interview, I opened the door and bowed. The bright sun silhouetted the interviewers against the windows. On the table, I saw the cedar boxes containing my paintings. They lay untouched.

I had asked the box maker to provide woven silk straps. To hide my ignorance from the professors, I had him teach me to tie the pentagonal knot traditionally used for artwork.

The knots were tight and difficult to undo. I set up the green-silver paintings. They appeared as sunlight shining through ocean water.

"What kind of paint did you use?"

"I used only silver," I replied. "The color is where it's tarnished. That's why both the silvery parts and the colored places glow."

"You've had quite a year. Did you enjoy yourself?"

I bowed in reply.

Kayama sensei continued. "We've been watching the progress on your paintings all year. Before making a decision, we needed to know that the paintings you submitted were actually painted by you. Ordinarily, we can't accept anyone without talking directly to every reference. But we didn't know how to communicate with your Professor Gilliam."

Professor Kayama turned and motioned to the paintings. "This innovation of yours ... by the way, it's quite good."

I bowed more deeply this time. Did this mean I was in?

———————

At the main office of the telephone company, I scheduled an international call home to report the possibility.

PURVEYORS OF JOY

When *I mixed my own paints, before coming* to Japan, I could get only chemical pigments with plastic-looking colors. Labeled with ratings of their various degrees of permanence—or lack thereof—they were graded according to how long they lasted under harsh light. But none were guaranteed to be totally permanent.

The area around Ueno, the park where the university is located, is unique. It contains four of the 10 stores that specialize in nihonga pigments in all of Japan.

I had been unceremoniously ushered out of the first store I'd visited there.

The fidgety man in the gray cardigan said he wouldn't sell to amateurs. He would only sell to the highest-ranking nihonga artists, such as Hirayama and Higashiyama, who had received the Emperor's Order of Cultural Merit.

But fortunately, I had found the wonderful pigment shop, Kinkai-do, with its owner, Sugita-san, who was friendly and helpful with my questions. The pigments I found—such as agates, jaspers, obsidian, and cinnabar—were amazing. Made of minerals straight from nature, the colors wouldn't fade.

From a fellow student, I learned of another pigment shop across Shinobazu pond from Ueno Park where the university is located. It is operated by the Matsushita family, and it is called *Kiya*, meaning "Purveyors of Joy."

My friend said some pigments were especially reasonable, but he added a cryptic warning that the shop might not be to my taste.

After I arrived at the shop and chose my pigments, a cheerful old woman in a pink sweater spooned them out of glass bottles onto the scales.

I heard a loud rumbling that caused the foundations of the building to shake as if a subway was passing underneath. But why was the sound coming from overhead? It didn't appear to trouble the woman, and her son continued labeling and sealing plastic envelopes. As I waited for my pigments, she grumbled under her breath. Was it about something I had done? Then I noticed her son, Mitsuru, looked angry and agitated. It was only after a few visits that I realized this discord was simply how they got along. It also explained to me why my friend had warned me that the store might not be to my taste.

I visited the shop one rainy day and found Mrs. Matsushita there alone. The drizzle had turned into a squall, and I waited inside for it to blow over. During our visit, we developed a pleasant relationship.

She shared memories of a time after World War II, when even

famous artists had to exchange paintings for pigment.

I grew to appreciate the Matsushita family and their business. I learned from her that their earlier store on that spot was built by her father in the 19th century, during the cultural flowering of the Meiji emperor's reign.[17] Over time, I became accustomed to ongoing squabbles between mother and son.

When her husband was there, the quibbling doubled. But after knowing them for a while, I realized there was no real animosity between them. With me, they were always extremely pleasant and showed interest in whatever exhibitions I was having.

I looked at thousands of bottles with poetic labels such as Dragon Sand, Underside of Willow Leaf, Silver Mouse, and Ibis Tail. Plants and birds featured prominently in those names. Malachite is called *Peacock Stone* in Japanese.

The methods for creating pigments are not written down. Families pass down techniques by word of mouth so rivals can't learn their secrets. The mass-produced paints of Western painting were easier for my generation of impatient and impecunious painters. And as a result, the Matsushita's customers were dwindling. They appreciated the fact that I was a regular visitor and so eager to learn anything I could from them. If I didn't visit them for a while, they welcomed me enthusiastically and jokingly said they thought I had returned to my home country.

---

17   The Tokugawa clan of shoguns had been granted the authority to govern by the emperor. But by 1868, the shogun, Tokugawa Yoshinobu, was no longer able to govern Japan and returned the license to govern back to the emperor. The emperor at the time was Mutsuhito, known as the Meiji emperor. With the government restored to the emperor, the feudal system was modernized to a constitutional democratic monarchy. With that, Japan opened its doors to the West for the first time in centuries. The reign of the Meiji emperor ended with his death in 1912. Andrew Gordon, *A Modern History of Japan* (New York: Oxford University, 2003).

THOROUGHLY

Finally, the day arrived for the university to post admissions. This time, I didn't think I could handle rejection alone. Mami took the day off to come with me. Again, I hid the engagement ring in my pocket, and we walked to the call board together to see if my number was there. The scroll was unfurled. Would I be on the list? I searched the columns for my number. Was that mine? No, that was for printmaking. What about nihonga? There it was!

Yes, I had been accepted.

We walked to the edge of Sanshiro Pond and sat on the rocks under a canopy of trees. I launched into an impassioned discourse about how difficult those years had been as we waited for this day, my plans for the future, and how I thought we could make things work with my career.

I left absolutely none of my feelings or plans unsaid.

When satisfied that I had expressed every ounce of persuasion that was in me, I finally fell to one knee and slipped the ring on her finger.

I had talked for so long that it was now too dark to see.

"What?" she asked. "Tell me what it's like. I can't see."

"Was that a *yes*?"

"Yes. Of course, it's a *yes*." We went under a streetlight so she could see the ring.

———

When hearing of the engagement, friends asked her, "So how did he propose?"

She said, "Thoroughly."

BILLBOARD WHO?

I **was visiting galleries with a slide-o-scope, which I** used to show slides of my work. I had little success. I found they always had a ready excuse for a brush-off. The galleries that showed contemporary work considered nihonga too old-fashioned for them. Galleries specializing in nihonga felt only the Japanese were entitled to create it. And they wouldn't meet with anyone under the age of 60.[18]

One gallery suggested I might talk to the American embassy. Did I know they had a collection of art? I did not.

I looked up the cultural attaché, and we arranged a meeting. The embassy needed artwork because they were redecorating. He liked my work but said, to be brutally honest, my work wasn't American

---

18   This is an especially interesting and unusual aspect of the nihonga world. As of this writing, I am months away from my 60th birthday, and I wonder what, if any, effect it might have.

enough. The whole point of the embassy's collection was to promote a certain red, white, and true-blue kind of American image abroad. Plant life as subject matter was just too Asian. Why not submit to Japanese galleries instead?

He had put me back at square one.

However, on the way home, I thought about what he said. They needed art because they were redecorating. Perhaps I should talk to interior designers. So, I made some small photo albums and took them to various interior designers' offices.

Around this time, I started to get some inquiries. It was clear the projects they brought to me for my consideration had been rejected by more than a few artists. Either the budget was too tight, or the deadline was impossibly close.

Nevertheless, in collaboration with these architects and interior designers, I experimented with creative ways to approach these challenging projects. That way, the best painting for the space could be achieved within their constraints. It became an excellent opportunity to creatively experiment with materials and techniques and to grow and mature as an artist.

One day I got a call from the director of the television program *Tokyo Mono*. Would I be interested in an interview? Sure, why not?

For three days, they filmed almost every facet of my life. They showed my rooms at the boardinghouse and the paintings I had used to decorate it. They interviewed my landlord and even the bath attendant at the public bath I went to every day.

I would have 30 minutes of airtime on Tokyo television—prime time! Allan West, nihonga painter. This would be my big break!

The program was to air while I was in the States getting married.

So, I bought an answering machine for my telephone and told the producers I would be happy to have them share my number with anyone who tried to contact me.

When we returned to Tokyo, the phone was full of messages, and a video of the television program had also been delivered. We were disappointed by the video. We noticed that, instead of focusing on my artwork, it was about the daily life of an exotic foreigner who just happened to be me.

We turned to the answering machine. All the messages were from the same person—a fellow called Takahashi, who had recently set up his own company. He had worked for a major ad agency but quit because he considered some of their practices unethical.

He had just landed an account with a warehouse corporation. It was a new division, and they wanted him to do the whole thing, including an inaugural ad campaign. The division was for the storage of art, for which ordinary facilities are often inadequate. They would meet the special requirements of temperature and humidity and also planned to add a viewing room and photographic studio to meet the needs of this growing clientele.

Takahashi-san wanted to use my art for this new ad blitz. I could hardly believe my good fortune! This would be a dramatic, career-making event.

We spoke on the phone for almost three hours. He chose his words carefully as he asked my feelings about a variety of issues. I saw art more as a matter of personal taste than as a commodity to market. His philosophy of introducing rather than selling agreed with my own. It was less of an audition and more the beginning of a friendship. We arranged a meeting.

I went to visit his office, not knowing what to expect. He was a thin, long-haired, craggy-faced man with a sheaf of papers and samples. He was the brains of the group as well as the writer of copy. He had a great team that included an impressive graphic designer.

He wanted to see my paintings, not just photographs of them. After a lot of brainstorming and visits to see my work, he hired a phenomenal photographer and lighting crew. We met in an aircraft hangar he rented as a photo studio.

A 14-foot-long screen painting was the one he had singled out. His crew of carpenters attached it to a large frame they had created for that purpose and suspended it from the ceiling with pulleys.

That was when I saw the entirety of his plan. I didn't know I was to be included in the photos, with the painting suspended behind me. He had hired a hair and makeup artist who made my hair look spiky. Takahashi-san had brought out an odd-looking jacket he wanted me to wear, which would fade out of sight unobtrusively in the photograph.

Takahashi-san wanted a sense of motion. They propped me up on a platform so the photographer could shoot from below. After tying a black string to the far corner of the painting, the assistant was to swing it in the air. I was concerned not only for the safety of the painting but also whether its swinging would topple me from the platform.

I was to take on a variety of expressions, everything from amusement to haughty disregard—to look left then right, to contemplate fictional things in the distance beyond the camera, to make a big smile then a faint one. Then I was to stare down the camera but not glare.

When the final layout and copy was finished, it was used for a series of eye-catching and colorful full-page magazine advertisements, billboards, and posters mounted in trains.

For almost a year, I had fun riding the trains, frequently seated under one of the posters. Never once was I recognized even by people who knew me. After all, what are the chances the person sitting under the poster could be the same one pictured in it? Besides, according to some people, "all foreigners look alike."

Less than a year after the ad campaign, the warehouse corporation failed. It was an interesting adventure at the time, but it never brought about an exhibition or a sale.

I remembered Professor Bruce Carter who had some experience exhibiting in Japan. He said, "They'll chew you up and spit you out if they don't ignore you completely."

SPOOKED

One hot summer's day in Tokyo, an epiphany moment came to me. It occurred at the magazine rack of an English bookstore in Ginza. I was leafing through the latest issue of *Art News* and saw an article that shook my world.

The article, called "Spook Art," by David Wise was an exposé of freshly declassified CIA documents all related to secret operations in the postwar era—in the art world involving American artists. It showed how the CIA worked behind the scenes to shift the cultural center of the art world's creative innovation from Europe to the United States. It was a campaign developed to firmly root such an impression in the public's mind. This was not because the CIA had a special love for art. The CIA had been motivated by a Cold War impulse to show America's brand of freedom in contrast to the U.S.S.R.'s repression. The CIA used American art and artists as its pawns in this war.

The documents claimed the most respected critics were specifically paid to write glowing reviews praising American artists in sharp contrast to European artists. The CIA also secretly funneled millions of dollars through known collectors and wealthy citizens to fund high-profile exhibitions. They presented these works as fresh and compelling—pioneering, avant-garde breakthroughs.

European artists were described as hopelessly passé and incapable of such innovation. They were denigrated as hampered by historical influence, academic aestheticism, and a melancholic Freudian psychology. Supposedly, this adversely affected their work.

The row of florescent lights hummed above me as sweat rolled down my back. I needed time to absorb this information. It was like a gut punch, and I stood there for a moment trying to catch my breath.

I looked at the back cover. Import duties and markups made it impossible for me to buy it and also pay for the subway home. It didn't matter. The caustic nature of the article had indelibly seared itself into my memory.

I knew this was going to have a profound effect on my attitude and my work going forward. But I had no way of knowing how. A clammy feeling spread out from my stomach.

Here in Tokyo, with the magazine in my hands, I suddenly saw my former artistic aspirations as a sham. I was in my 30s, yet I felt like a child learning Santa Claus was a malicious fraud. All abstract expressionist painters—Jackson Pollock, who had been a particular hero of mine, Robert Motherwell, Franz Klein, Mark Rothko—all had a strength and a confidence I admired. And yet now I felt I had been duped.

With this short article, my allegiance to modernism broke. I lost the need to tether myself to the artistic modes of my age. I could now see it as one of the many influences that I could draw on if needed. But my earlier sense of modernism's superiority and my blindness to most other available influences disappeared.

I had thought these men pioneered a new aesthetic, and I'd wanted to join them and add my part to the forward movement of art history. Now I would need to rethink my values and my aspirations. And how should I deal with galleries and institutions going forward?

To me, modernism was now suspect and the malformed result of decades of concerted manipulation. I wanted no part of it. But if I rejected abstraction and modernism in my art, it meant galleries were less likely to show my work. It would be harder to sell paintings and harder to make a living.

It meant independence, but was I willing to sacrifice the security of having a gallery promote and sell my work? I would also be unappealing to art critics the minute I was no longer edgy or challenging.

But the thought of applying such tricks of the trade to get attention became sickening. If I continued playing with abstraction, I would lose all interest in painting. It was time for me to start on my own, creating a pure aesthetic based on what I personally liked best.

I had reached the point of no return.

The paintings I was about to show a museum's curator were part of an aesthetic I would now have to abandon. How could I discuss them honestly now that my feelings about them had changed?

I would have to dig down deeper into my studies. I had expected to learn the traditional brushwork techniques of the Kano and Rimpa school at the university but was disappointed to discover nihonga had instead become westernized—by eliminating the historical Asian linework.

I began visiting used bookstores, searching through rare wood-block and traditionally bound books. I persisted, and once in a great while, here and there, I was able to find Kano school textbooks.

My need to express the sacred in nature drove my experiments with paint. I would learn from these texts how to add the necessary vibrancy through fluid lines.

I eventually filled a bookcase with Kano textbooks that had been used centuries before. The study of these has occupied me through the years. The Japanese phrase *on ko chi shin* means "by being rooted in the past, we can come to understand the new." This was going to be my new model, a replacement for the "cult of the new" that modernism had become.

NAME VALUE

An architect approached me for a possible commission. He had almost completed a concert hall and needed a mural to hang opposite the main entrance, front and center.

He couldn't find an artist to paint it for the life of him.

He had gone over budget, and because the funds for artwork had been allocated elsewhere, every other artist had rejected the job as paying too little. There was neither adequate time to find a new painter nor the time needed for an artist to complete the work.

I asked what the budget was, and the number knocked the wind out of me. It wouldn't even pay for half the materials.

I was to give him my decision that night.

Mami and I were at the end of our rope. I needed work, but I couldn't accept a job that would put us even further behind.

How could I make a profit from a budget of half the amount I needed for the materials? Mami suggested that I calculate carefully how much it would cost to make the mural. It needed to be huge, as the building was a postmodern interpretation of the Pantheon.

I went to the studio. Looking up, I could see the silver vinyl reflecting panels I had installed across my ceiling. I wondered about the size and got on a ladder to measure them. Three panels together would be just right.

I would need sturdy paper to adhere to the wooden panels. An extra wide roll of high-quality mulberry paper I had been saving would be perfect. If the size was right, this might be just the time for it. I had barely enough for three panels.

Rummaging around in the studio, I found some copper leaf. It had been left over from a project after miscalculating the amount I needed. It should go well with the terra-cotta color of the concert hall interior.

I found a bag of chemical pigments from when I was in the States. If I limited my colors to those with the highest permanency rating, I could keep down costs while maintaining stability and beauty.

After careful calculations, I would at least be able to pay for family living expenses while working on the project. Maybe a new commission would materialize in the meantime.

I got Mami's hesitant okay. Because of the recognition he promised I was to receive, we were assured that it would lead to other, better projects. When I gave my assent to the architect, he was a bit surprised but also relieved.

"Oh, great! Thanks. I'll make sure you get proper recognition for this."

I spent that night ripping the silver vinyl off the panels and dampening the paper for stretching. Once the paper was stretched and primed, I laid down the copper leaf. Each panel was a full-day marathon. I tarnished the copper into a nice verdigris color in places, then painted leaves—lots and lots of leaves, a wall full of green leaves.

I ran out of green paint. Okay, now for some blue leaves. To add a divine spark, I painted the spirit of the forest in two huge sweeping strokes of maroon. It had been a challenge, but I was pleased with the results and certain it would look splendid in its new home.

I framed it and put it on the truck to install the day before the ribbon-cutting ceremony.

For public artwork like this, the client normally requests the title of the painting ahead of time. That way they can create a caption plate for the wall. This time, the client was a local government, and I knew they were busy. So, on the day of installation, I went to the manager of the facility to tell him what title should be printed on the caption plate.

When I found him, he was standing before the painting and admiring it in a proprietary manner.

Seeing me approach, he said in careful English, "No. We are not open."

A bit too loud, he then pronounced his words slowly as if to a child, "Not. Open. Now," and turned away. He appeared to be looking for a guard to get rid of this foreigner.

I thought a wave of fluent Japanese might put him at ease. So, speaking now to his back, I addressed him. "Good afternoon, and excuse me, sir. Let me introduce myself. I'm Allan West, the painter of this mural you were just looking at." I continued. "May I ask you a question or two?"

The manager turned. Tugging on the bottom of his vest, he hesitated and asked, "May I help you?"

"Yes, thank you. No one has contacted me yet about the wall caption. I wondered to whom I should speak regarding this issue. Might you be the right gentleman to tell me?"

"*You* painted that?" He pointed to my mural.

"Yes, I did. I installed it just this morning."

He avoided making eye contact with me but called the architect over. "Did you commission ..."—and indicating my direction, he cleared his throat—"to paint this mural?"

"Yes, sir, I did, and it's an excellent job! Don't you agree?"

"Sure, of course," the manager said. "It is." He glanced at the painting and spoke under his breath. "But do you really think he painted it?"

I broke in. "Yes, I did."

"Well, then." He turned to leave.

"Shall I give you the information for the wall caption?"

He dismissed me by saying, "There won't be any wall caption. This is a *public* facility." And with that explanation, the conversation was over.

I didn't understand. It seemed particularly odd, as I had never heard of a public facility that did *not* credit the artist by name.

The architect followed the manager back to his office to explain. I could see by their body language that it would be of no use.

As I was about to leave, a sculptor who was installing his work beside the entrance asked me if I was planning to go to the opening ceremony the next day. I said I hadn't been invited. Perhaps it was an oversight.

I decided to go home. It was a dark, moonless night, and I got lucky. A taxi stopped for me. The driver and I had an amiable discussion for about 15 minutes. He didn't realize he had a foreigner in the back seat. He asked what I did for a living. When I told him I was a nihonga painter, he said he had heard a rumor there was a *foreigner* somewhere in the area who *also* did nihonga.

I said, "That's me."

He whipped his head around and stopped the cab. "When did *you* get in!"

Even though I continued speaking Japanese, I couldn't convince him I was the fare he had picked up—the one with whom he had been speaking.

The next evening, I went back to see what the concert hall looked like without the plastic sheeting protecting the floors. I could take a photograph for promotional purposes. At the entrance, I gave my name to the attendant. She couldn't find my name anywhere on the list.

The architect saw me leaving and offered to take me in through a side door. The facilities were bustling with activity. People were standing before my mural, admiring it, so I couldn't get an unobstructed photograph. I would have to check again later. Meanwhile, I walked around to see the rest of the cultural center.

I soon heard the architect call my name. He was inviting me to enter the auditorium for the opening ceremony. I thanked him but said I would wait until everyone was inside, so I could take a photograph of my painting. I would join him after that.

I took a few photos, then noticed a gallery off to the side. In it were displays of calligraphy by elementary and junior high school students taped to the wall around the gallery. Their characters for *world peace* and *traditional culture* were almost identical to each other.

Beside each example was a carefully printed caption giving the name, age, and school of the artist.

Well, *some* artists got wall captions!

NEVER SO ALONE

The concert hall project ended, and no further commissions materialized. I realized that being a foreigner in this job was going to be more of an impediment that I had originally thought. I would need to be more proactive in promoting my art, not just making it.

Under the circumstances, I had feared marriage. It would require too much work and privation just to get by as an artist. Art history is full of such stories. I didn't want to put anyone else through that ordeal, and yet Mami said she felt her fate was to help me succeed.

After three years of dating, our lives had become thoroughly entwined. She knew what to expect and was sure of me. If she didn't fear for our future, why should I? The economy was encouraging and gave us a sense that the future was going to be glorious.

Then almost immediately after our marriage began, construction sites went silent; buildings stood dark and cold; weeds grew in empty lots. This was the beginning of Japan's disastrous Lost Decade.

I still painted, but it wasn't going well. I was just able to keep the exhibitions in the black, but little was left for living. After all expenses were paid, we could barely exist on the crusts of the exhibitions. Was this just a slump?

While I spent hours in the studio, I was usually alone. Mami was too busy to visit the studio anymore. At least, that's what I thought. I missed the conversations we had when I was working—the way she encouraged me to take risks and be venturesome with my brush.

I doubted I could survive by creating the art I liked. Desperate to generate more sales, I returned to modernism. Applying what I had once rejected, I synthesized those shapes, conceptualized relationships within the composition and, within that construct, placed forms with a palpable presence and all such modernist gobbledygook. But because of this, I no longer enjoyed painting.

I needed the light Mami always brought to the studio. Hoping she could help me figure out what was wrong—get me out of the slump—I invited her to the studio one day.

She said, "I don't like to go. I can't stand to see the art that's responsible for all my misery."

I knew she wasn't happy, but this was beyond my comprehension. Could I successfully navigate this marriage of two cultures?

She had lost faith in me when I most needed her encouragement and anticipation.

I had never felt so alone as I did in the studio that night.

THE PRICE OF ADMISSION

"**Y**ou know, Allan, you would be perfect for this."

I was in Kinkaido, my favorite pigment store. The owner, my good friend Sugita-san, handed me a pamphlet. It was calling for a preliminary sketch as a proposal for a public project in a nearby prefecture.

I read through the pamphlet. The subject matter was the elegance of nature and the four seasons. That was right up my alley. I agreed with Sugita-san, that I probably had a good chance. The handling fee for submissions was rather steep for that sort of thing, but we both thought it was well worth it.

My tab at Kinkaido was getting a bit long, so maybe the purchase prize would help me pay off part of the tab—perhaps all of it.

For the entry, I put everything I had into my preliminary sketch. In fact, it was a sparkling miniature painting of what I was proposing to the committee—intertwined cherry blossoms bursting on silver leaf and vibrant green and crimson maple leaves on gold.

I was soon informed that my painting was a finalist. I would have the results any day.

I finally received the news. "We regret to inform you that the competition committee has chosen to take the project along a different route. After much deliberation, we have decided that an artist who is native to this prefecture will be a better choice." I didn't read further.

Later that year, I was in the area and thought I'd stop by to see what I could learn from seeing the painting they had chosen.

It did not match the theme of the elegance of nature and the four seasons.

I asked around and learned that, with this sort of thing, the members of the selection committee usually jockey for power. The winner of this struggle then overrides the majority vote and awards the prize to one of their own protégées.

I understood applicants were expected to ply the committee members with New Year's gifts, bulging envelopes, and so on to make it worth their while. I did not want to contribute to the system of that shady world.

Mami and I were getting desperate. I needed to find some way of getting my name out there. I remembered the concert hall I had painted for and wondered whether perhaps someone other than that confrontational manager noticed that there was no caption on my painting that hangs there, front and center. I prepared for the visit. It was a weekday afternoon. I could probably enter without being seen by too many people. As I had suspected, though captions were beside all the other artwork, mine was still bereft. I had come prepared with paint to put in a proper signature. It took some time to get a sense of the flow of people in and out of the atrium. I found my opportunity and whipped out the paint and my brush, and in large katakana that could be seen from across the room, I signed the painting. It would have to be the advertising I sorely needed.

On the way home, I decided to stop by the office that had set up the competition for public artwork on the theme of the elegance of nature. Perhaps there would be another project that needed artwork on a similar theme. Hanging on the wall of the vestibule was my painting that I had submitted as a preliminary sketch.

They had placed it in an expensive frame for their own enjoyment.

PARENTHOOD

In spite of setbacks and disappointments, Mami and I were over-joyed—we were going to be parents!

The impersonal approach of the hospitals we visited horri-fied Mami. She insisted on having me help with the birth, and none of the hospitals would allow me near her.

We chose a midwife named Kamiya-san, whom we mentioned only casually to our parents. Both sets of parents were absolutely against the idea. It would be necessary for me to run interference and somehow put them at ease.

They made me promise to register with a hospital. I did and paid the nonrefundable deposit we could ill afford. Nevertheless, as the due date approached, there was no way Mami could persuade the hospital to let me join her when the time came, so we cancelled.

One day, when I was buying pigments from Sugita-san, she presented us with a small round package of powdered kudzu wrapped like a protective amulet. She had bought it at a temple dedicated to expectant mothers. It is traditionally believed that drinking this guarantees a successful delivery.

The expected day came and went. Our parents called, wondering if Mami was packed for the hospital. I simply said we had done everything possible to prepare. In anticipation, I set up in our apartment a large folding-screen painting I had made of the primeval forest.

Kamiya-san had been monitoring our progress regularly. Two weeks passed, and the baby kept growing. I could tell how the baby was positioned from my days sketching the pregnant woman at Carnegie Mellon. This surprised Kamiya-san. I asked if we needed to worry, because sometimes the baby was head-side up. She said they almost always right themselves in time.

Late that night, the contractions began.

This time they were not like the phantom contractions Mami had had before. They were different, and we called Kamiya-san, who stopped by to reassure us.

She said she was delivering three babies all at the same time, but she would bicycle over again on her way back from another delivery nearby.

The contractions gradually went from 20 minutes to seven minutes and then five minutes.

I gripped the lintel as Mami laced her fingers together and hung from my neck, sometimes pulling her knees up to let gravity take its course.

We were interrupted by a phone call. It was my parents, and they asked eagerly. "Any news? We couldn't wait to hear from you."

"No, nothing to report so far." Then Mami let out a wail.

"What was that? Was that Mami?"

There was no denying it.

"Have the contractions started?" they asked. "How far apart are they?"

"Well, uh ... it's still quite early."

"You mean the hospital didn't tell you to come?"

"Not yet. Everything is progressing normally. That's what they say."

My parents were frantic. "Don't wait another second. You should go out and hail a cab!"

"All right, then I need to go."

We returned to our previous position. My calves bulged, and my arms strained. I knew my pain was nothing compared to what Mami was suffering. I must not let her sense my fear.

Hours later, her cries were no longer the regular sounds of child-birth. They seemed urgent and suddenly beyond human capability—then low and weak, like the sound of someone dying.

In a panic, I called Kamiya-san, who came quickly. Just one look at Mami, pale and limp on the futon, and she expressed urgent concern. Mami wasn't dilating fast enough and seemed to have lost all strength. She would need energy, but the last series of pushes must not happen until her body was ready. Between contractions, Mami would need to recover.

Kamiya-san gave her some of the kudzu[19] tea Sugita-san had given us, and Mami revived visibly. Her grip tightened. The color and

---

19   Kudzu tea is made from the starchy roots of the kudzu vine. It is subtly sweet and refreshing when served cold in the summer. Hot kudzu tea is also nice in the winter.

determination returned to her face.

Before long, little Ray was born. With a cough and a sputter, he took his first breath.

It had been 26 hours. Exhausted,[20] the three of us slept beneath the *Primeval Forest*

We called our parents with the news. My parents were overjoyed. "Imagine not being able to hail a cab at that time of day. And what a fantastic coincidence that you had a midwife right there in the neighborhood! It's wonderful she could take over."

Before our sons Gen and Rick were born, my parents made us promise to call on Kamiya-san to deliver them as well.

Sugita-san presented us with packets of kudzu each time.

---

20 Kamiya-san asked for a sushi knife. It is not so common anymore, but traditionally, midwives would prepare the placenta as sushi and serve it to the exhausted couple for energy. It tasted like liver.

ROGUE'S GALLERY

That summer we took our newborn to see his grandparents. I decided to visit some galleries in Washington, DC, while I was there. I found a beautiful brownstone gallery in Georgetown that I knew had shown Professor Gilliam's work. Additionally, they exhibited Asian things and colorful patterned artwork as well. It would be a good match for me. I called and got an appointment.

I went to Grandby's Gallery,[21] and the woman who opened the door said Mr. Grandby was not there yet, but he was on his way. We went down to the lower level. I showed her my work and answered her questions. She was enthusiastic.

She qualified all her comments with the fact that she had no authority or influence over who was or was not chosen.

Forty-five minutes passed. Mr. Grandby still had not appeared.

---

21   I have changed the name of this gallery and its owner.

She looked at her watch. "Let me show you some of the fun artists we're showing." She moved to a white chest of drawers to show me patterned pieces, colorful works on paper.

"He likes these, so I expect him to like yours even more."

This was encouraging.

When it was an hour and a half past the appointed time, I felt awkward about her having to entertain me and thought it would be best to leave and reconnect at a different time. I was just gathering my belongings when there was a loud sound upstairs. Her lips tightened. Was this her husband?

We went up to greet him. Mr. Grandby was tipsy and leaned his flabby body precariously against the doorjamb for support.

She introduced me in soothing tones. "Grandby, this is your appointment—Allan West."

"No. No, no, no!" he snarled. "I'm not seeing anybody."

It had been a pleasant meeting until then.

"But you invited him to come at five o'clock."

"Tough. I've just been to a bunch of openings. They're all crap."

"Yes, but I know you'll like these." She was not making any headway. "Or shall I reschedule the appointment? He's been waiting for an hour and a half."

"Hell no."

He clutched the doorknob, glowering. "Look, kid, if you're still painting, try again in eight years." He waved me off with a meaty hand.

I could tell they had a history of tension and of her having to smooth his ruffled feathers. She ushered me out apologetically. I thanked her and left for the subway.

Shaken, I waited for the train and thought, Eight years? Why *eight* years, Mr. Grandby? You'll wish you signed me up when you had the chance!

THE MOST IMPOSSIBLE CLIENT IN ALL OF TOKYO

An interior designer approached me after hearing I* was the artist of last resort. Would I paint a forest scene?

The president of a well-known corporation needed her to design an apartment for his secret love affairs. I would need to be discreet. The man had a reputation for being the most impossible client to work with in all of Tokyo. He had already cut ties with several prestigious design firms.

The interior designer had already spent more time finding art for him than on everything else put together. She needed to keep his account, but he rejected all the artwork presented to him. He couldn't articulate what he wanted—only that whatever was presented to him was impossibly ugly.

The time for his occupancy was approaching, and he still had not approved any artwork. Shipping and returning paintings for approval had eaten into her budget. Artists were now refusing to even send photographs. The designer knew I was one of the rare artists who took commissions, and she contacted me in desperation. Perhaps I could help her figure out what he wanted.

She was no longer able to pay very much but wondered if I would meet with the man.

It was a hard decision for Mami and me, because the bills were piling up. I couldn't risk complications or delays with the designer's tight budget, and yet I was confident I could give satisfaction.

Upon meeting the man, I sensed his frustration. He hated muddy-looking paintings. We flipped through some photographs of my work and discussed his impressions to figure out what he wanted.

He pointed to the photo of one painting and said that was what he wanted, but in the appropriate size. It wouldn't require any labor-intensive gold leaf work, so I could finish it on time.

I carefully matched the colors with the painting he had seen in the photograph. When the time came to install it, he took one look at the painting and told me the colors were different. They didn't work for him.

The designer looked crestfallen. I couldn't afford to lose her trust, so I needed her client to be satisfied.

For her, it was simply one more rejection. For me, the expenses of the commission, which I could ill afford, were coming out of my pocket.

I realized the color of the photograph he liked was different from the actual painting I had tried to replicate.

I went out on a limb and said, "I guarantee to give you a painting you'll love wholeheartedly. I'll do whatever it takes."

"In that case, I want it in a fresh green like this," he said. He pointed to the designer's *light-blue handbag.*

I exchanged a glance with the designer. She appeared completely nonplussed. But now *I* understood what had to be done. I told the man, "I love working with a client who knows what he likes. Let me get some materials together for your approval. Could we meet again tomorrow?"

Outside, the designer looked upset and turned to me. "What were you doing in there?"

"Don't worry," I said. "I figured out the problem—he's color-blind. Leave it to me."

I purchased samples of all the greens and browns I thought would work and showed them to him the next day. After comparing them carefully, he approved four of the greens and three of the browns.

I completed and installed the painting just in time for the interior design firm to turn over the apartment to the praise of their newly won client.

I would need to find a buyer for the painting he had rejected. Otherwise, it would be difficult to feed my new family.

I had successfully painted for the most impossible client in Tokyo. It hadn't been easy, but I learned from the challenge.

RISK DUMPING

A *t one time, kings, nobles, and popes had* lavish palaces with extensive art collections. Cathedrals had art that emphasized the line of papal succession or divine approbation. In both Japan and in the West, art justified the power and authority of ruling classes, whether religious or secular.

The Flemish painter Peter Paul Rubens's work in this vein was so popular with the 17th-century European elite that he became one of the wealthiest men of his age. This meant he was called upon to broker diplomatic relations between Spain and England, and it was even rumored he bailed out a failing European state.

In Japan, the shoguns[22] had lavish palaces fitted with artwork that supported their legitimacy as the emperor's authorized rulers. Buddhist temples had vast collections of art depicting the ideals of the

---

22 Shoguns were the hereditary officials who governed Japan for eight centuries until 1868.

pure land—the heaven where parishioners hoped to one day dwell.

The works of art were taken from their enormous warehouses to dry in the autumn air. This gave the citizenry a special opportunity to see art otherwise unavailable for public enjoyment. They were charged a fee. To this day, the Japanese consider autumn the season to enjoy art.

When we think of the traditional museum today, even if it is not the vestige of a fallen monarchy, the architecture tends to be palatial.

Just as the Louvre Museum and the Hermitage were once royal palaces, in the West, other palaces and their art collections became property of the state when monarchies fell.

Even now, a museum begins when a significant collection of art leaves the hands of its wealthy owner and needs a home. Most Japanese don't know Japan's National Museum is actually the imperial collection that was donated to the public.[23]

Until the 19th century, due to the high cost of materials, artists painted by order of those who could pay. The European artist and the Japanese Kano artist operated on a studio, or workshop, system somewhat like a guild. Masters took in disciples who were required to assist them in exchange for lessons as well as room and board.

From the 18th century to the mid-19th century, European salons and academies were established. Artists who were voted into a salon by other artists would pool their resources to hold an annual or semiannual exhibit. Works were chosen by juries of the salon's organizational hierarchy.

An exhibited painting would be sold through the organization,

23 こんなに面白い東京国立博物館 April 21, 2005 新潮社.

and the organization would determine which artist would be the recipient of a patron's commission. This was a way for an artist to gain exposure, notoriety, or a reputation—and make a living.

A salon was careful to maintain the quality and the image it presented. Not having a painting in the salon show could severely affect one's income. And the cohesive determination of the jury usually stifled artists into painting in ways that would ensure their acceptance.

Academies were like salons in structure, but the leadership also instructed the others. Through this instruction, the average artist was channeled into learning exactly what his teacher would require for acceptance into a coming exhibition.

This was a stultifying pressure. When we refer to art with the pejorative term *academic*, it reflects this history rather than any scholarly effort on the artist's part.

In late-19th-century Japan, after the government was restored to the emperor, this Western concept of the salon and the academy were introduced to Japan. Though it has all but disappeared in the West, the tradition exists in Japan to this day. My studio is surrounded by a variety of these academies.

My professor, Kayama Matazo, was in the top hierarchy of the Sogakai salon, one block away. I was expected to submit a painting to the jury twice a year and pay dues as a disciple of the man decorated with the Imperial Order of Culture. I could see no particular benefit in participation. It was mostly out of respect for Kayama sensei and to do what was expected.

In the 1940s, Peggy Guggenheim, the New York socialite, art

collector, and gallery owner,[24] gave artists a monthly stipend and a percentage of everything she sold.[25] I understood this was standard. Gallery owners had a vested interest in the continued health and well-being of the artist and the continued production of art.

After that, the art world shifted slightly, and a gallery promised to buy all an artist's production for that year, selling it and keeping all the profit, whatever that may be.

A larger shift came when the gallery would guarantee a certain amount of work would sell, and a percentage of whatever sold beyond that would also go to the artist.

Notice where the risk shifted with each change. A little later, a gallery would promise so many shows a year and give the artist 70% of the sales. All discounts came out of the gallery's percentage.

Gradually the artist's percentage shrank smaller and smaller. Fifty percent became standard. It was difficult to make a living exhibiting at only one gallery, forcing artists to juggle exhibits with more than one gallery.

This led galleries to impose exclusivity contracts, insisting that an artist exhibit with them and none other. As a result, an artist's full year's living might be determined by the whims of only one gallery owner's single exhibition. The risk was gradually and progressively transferred to the artist without noticeable objection. We artists depended on galleries and weren't able to conceive of any other way to do business.

24 Peggy Guggenheim (1898–1979) was a large figure in avant-garde art. She championed European surrealists after WWII, especially in New York City and Venice. She gave Jackson Pollock his first major commission and solo exhibitions and provided him with a stipend for five years.
25 Stephen Naifeh and Gregory W. Smith, *Jackson Pollock: An American Saga* (New York: Clarkson Potter, 1989).

Yet another trend emerged during the 1980s. Hoping for an easy income from real estate, people who were not especially interested in art were the ones to operate a new kind of rental gallery without curation or promotion. In turn, they let artists rent the empty space on a weekly basis. Some maintained the original florescent lighting and carpet tiles from their earlier incarnation as office space.

What could go wrong? The art world avoided artists who exhibited in them, as they were considered vanity galleries.

Japan's economic downturn in the '90s caused many of the most serious galleries to close their doors, and the vanity gallery became a part of the scene more than ever.

One night on prime-time television, Mami and I saw a politician touting the New National Museum of Art as a beacon to the world and a symbol of Japan's art scene. The New Museum does not even have a permanent collection and is essentially another piece of real estate available for rent. So, sadly, the New Museum *is* symbolic of Japan's art scene, but in the worst way possible.

With insidious progression, the vanity gallery broke down all re-sistance to this kind of vanity museum. By manipulating the criteria for usage, even trade shows for mass-produced foreign electronics have been presented there as works of art. And they have done so under the flimsiest of disguises.

Ironically, in the succeeding years, genuine art galleries pre-sented progressively more and more off-putting art while hoping to legitimize the curators as edgy. As a result, they are making the gallery a less welcoming place.

Sadly, whatever it takes to alienate an art fanatic, potential patron, or even artist, too many galleries are doing it with great efficiency.

THE WEIGHT OF GENERATIONS

Mr. Furuichi came to my studio. He was corporate president of his family business, and his friendly manner was the product of 150 years of history. Yet his urgency surprised me.

He brought with him a can of their nori seaweed. Without a doubt, it was the best nori I had eaten or could ever hope to eat. It was fragrant and delicious. I couldn't get enough of it.

There was no question as to its excellence. The Kabuki theater put its own logo on his product and sold it as a high-quality gift. The most venerable department store in Ginza presented it as their premium house brand. The most expensive banquet houses, where the top geisha entertained, chose this nori.

This company employs the most respected seaweed taster in Japan, and at the first auctions of the new harvest, he is given first refusal. In the 150 years of business, Mr. Furuichi's nori had always been chosen as, and used for, other brands and under other labels.

Then the president told me of his predicament.

Despite the universal recognition of the quality of his seaweed, he had never sold this nori under their own name. So, there was no brand recognition whatsoever. Orders from these other entities had become unreliable.

During this time, Italian foods were gaining in popularity. As a result, rice consumption was suddenly at an all-time low. And because nori is usually eaten folded around rice, seaweed sales were down.

For the first time, he needed to sell the seaweed under his own name. The future of the company was going to be at the mercy of this momentous decision, so sales must be successful.

Would I design the package?

I asked Mr. Furuichi all I could about the history of his company and the process of growing and harvesting nori. I felt a lot of pressure while listening to his explanations. Not only was the family's tradition hanging on this painting, but a lot of dearly preserved customs are also associated with the long history of Japan's seaweed culture.

The best-quality seaweed requires just the right temperature. Originally, seaweed was grown on bundles of sticks planted into the bed of the river's mouth. Depending on the weather, the temperature, and many other variables, the seaweed harvest could differ vastly from year to year.

Currently, nori nets are stretched within a narrow band of fresh water that must blend with ocean water at just the right percentage. These nets are not meant to catch the nori, but rather, they provide an armature onto which the seaweed grows.

Mr. Furuichi explained nori is also purchased to give guests at weddings and funerals. The package design would need to reflect not only the quality of the nori but also the formality of such occasions. Because seaweed is used as a Shinto offering, the use of it must follow certain customs.

The airtight can was to be about the size of a fat can of tennis balls, and I would have a degree of freedom in its design. I was also to design the wooden box in which it would be packaged.

The wooden box must have a cloth wrapping, which I was also to design.

There was a superstitious concern that the goodness inside a packaged gift might escape at the edges of the paper. For that reason, with traditional items and those dealing with ceremony or custom, the wrapping paper is folded carefully inside itself, at acute angles to avoid exposed edges.

According to Mr. Furuichi, the typical Western style of wrapping at right angles is called *caramel wrapping*, because it was introduced to Japan with the import of caramels. But the packaging of the nori would need to be done on a higher level of formality.[26] It would need a silk wrapping.

The most formal gift giving usually includes a carefully folded piece of hexagonal paper in red and white that contains a thinly stretched piece of dried abalone. The abalone represents a wish for prosperity for the receiver of the gift.

On the cover of the silk, I drew an abalone and had the pieces

---

26 There is great emphasis placed on presentation in Japanese culture. Aspects of this can be found in the traditional care given to packaging. One book that introduces this well is *How to Wrap Five Eggs: Traditional Japanese Packaging* by Hideyuki Oka.

form the word *nori*. Out from behind this, I painted a branch of plum blossoms, because it is only during the short period when plum trees blossom that the most delicious seaweed can be harvested. This was to represent the high quality.

Nightingales love the nectar of plum blossoms, so I placed one nightingale flying from the other edge of the wrapper.

On the wooden box, I painted a forest-green outline of a pine tree, and cherry blossoms, in a circular escutcheon. The short duration of their blooms suggested the transitory nature of life.

For the can, the foreground is a river; a spit of land is in the middle section, and the ocean is in the background. On careful inspection, you might see the bundled branches staked to the ocean bed. I made the plum tree most prominent and accentuated the name of the company by surrounding it with the branches. I was asked to write the lettering as well. Within the calligraphy is the name of the company hidden in parts of the word *seaweed*.

Furuichi-san delivered one can after another for my enjoyment as I worked. Seaweed became my snack of choice. Why bother wrapping the seaweed around rice? While painting in the middle of the night, I took it straight, like chips.

I felt increasingly motivated to create a painting worthy of his nori.

If I could make the can look especially exciting, I knew people would keep it, and it could serve as a lasting form of advertisement.

It became a garden of plants and flowers in all seasons, with fortuitous meanings and symbolism.

In the sky, I placed both a sun and a moon. I wanted to provide enough detail so that, after someone studied it a long time, there was still something new and interesting to see in it. To make that possible, I painted it on a large-scale screen.

Another plan I had was to disguise the seam of the painting so it would be difficult to locate on the cylinder of the can. To paint it that way, I folded the screen back on itself. Where the leftmost edge met the rightmost edge, I painted them together so the motif continued across both.

As I work, it helps to imagine the face of the person I'm painting for. And I picture the way the painting will be used. I always promise clients I'll work with them until they're completely satisfied. Throughout the process of painting, I become familiar with every inch of the painting as it develops and transforms. Each part of the painting must work for the benefit of the whole.

Whenever I don't feel completely confident, what do I see at night? I see a look of shock on the client's face, and silence while they try to figure out what to say. Would *that look* come over Mr. Furuichi's face? This time, if I should have to come up with something different at the last minute, the deadline would be brutal.

This was the most consequential project I had worked on so far, and yet I was afraid I might have totally missed the mark. I had done my research on seaweed and read books from the historical archives. But it would be entirely different from any other seaweed company's packaging on the market.

I spent a lot of time sitting above this painting, working from the bridge I built over it. Throughout months of looking down at the painting, it gradually materialized and came into focus.

At last, the painting was complete, and I couldn't think of anything else that might improve it. I could only hope it would meet the needs of the project.

I called Mr. Furuichi. He had been thinking of calling me and asked if he could come right away.

I frantically straightened up the studio and set up the screen. All the mess I couldn't put away in time was hidden behind the painting. I could see his silhouette at the front door. I turned on some quiet music and counted to three. I didn't want to run to the door or have him think that I was anxious, even though I was.

I probably should have changed clothes. I hoped he wouldn't think me rude. Oh well, it was too late. And it was an artist's studio, so it might not have come as a surprise.

I opened the door for him, and he presented me with a can of nori.

"Thank you! Yes, perfect timing."

After abbreviated small talk, I followed him to where the painting was waiting. He stepped forward, and I soon saw his shoulders rise—a sudden intake of breath, then nothing. There was a long, uncomfortable silence. I let him get his first impression. He'd need some time to decide how he wanted me to change it.

To keep from influencing his thinking, I withdrew a little.

He pulled out his handkerchief and raised it to his face. Was he stifling a sneeze?

His frame shuddered, and he said, "I'm sorry."

I realized he was overcome with emotion. Turning, he reached for my hand.

My relief was indescribable.

Instead of his usual restrained bow, I received an enthusiastic handshake, and I knew the weight of generations of nori sellers had been lifted.

"Finally," he said, "our own label—our own brand. We're going to be all right."

FROM SOCKS AND UNDERWEAR

A *certain Tokyo department store gallery persuaded me to* exhibit with them. They stressed how actively they would publicize the exhibition, and in a moment of weakness, I agreed to it.

They insisted that I provide all-new work. It was a tight deadline, but by cutting back on sleeping, eating, and other essential uses of time, I hoped to create a body of new work in time for the exhibition.

By the night of the hanging, I was exhausted. Despite that, I had to remind myself of how fortunate I was to benefit from such "incomparable publicity."

I soon discovered that incomparable publicity consisted of a sheet of paper on every other floor of the department store—visible to anyone who happened to come equipped with a powerful magnifying glass.

I would receive a generous 23% of the sales (minus the cost of incidentals such as tea, cakes, and incomparable publicity) while the gallery would take only the paltry sum that was left—77%.

In a happier turn of events, I was asked to introduce myself and my work to the gallery staff. I was to meet with them before they left for the evening. They looked like stewardesses but in tweed uniforms.

We spent an animated hour together, during which I fielded questions for the eager employees. In the end, I was confident each one had a thorough understanding of the techniques and materials I used, as well as my biography.

I felt a cold coming on, but I still had a lot of work to do after they all went home for the evening.

With great care, I arranged the works to best advantage—an imposing piece just opposite the entrance would make an impact from outside, and some of the more intimate works would show to better advantage in the closer areas of the gallery. I thought through balancing themes with color combinations as I had seen done at the Smithsonian.

At 3 a.m., I finally finished. Exhausted but relieved, I could go home to a long sleep. I was planning not to set an alarm; if I slept through the day, I just might be able to prevent this cold that was coming on.

On my way out, I shared the freight elevator with a gallery official. He told me that before he was assigned to the gallery, he had worked in men's socks and handkerchiefs, and his supervisor had been pleased with the improvement in sales during his tenure.

While showing me to the after-hours exit, he said he looked forward to seeing me every day during the coming week. I told him that, first and foremost, I would have to look after my health. The deadline of a commissioned work was looming.

"Well," he said, "we can't sell your work if you aren't in the gallery."

I had been expecting to sit in the gallery only the first and last days—that was part of the arrangement—but not throughout the whole exhibition.

He said, "I'll overlook tomorrow. Just come in when you wake up. You can be here the whole day for the rest of the week."

How could I possibly meet the deadline for the commission I needed to finish at my studio?

I arrived around noon the next day to find my works completely rearranged. My labors until three in the morning had been entirely in vain.

I asked why the paintings had been shuffled. The resulting explanation was unheard of, in my experience. The manager saw customers as somewhat dim-witted. He was sure they would be confused by the progression if the paintings were placed along the wall in *varied* sizes.

They had moved the large-sized paintings to one wall and the middle-sized ones to another. He pointed out how they had hung "all the cute little ones" together.

The socks-and-handkerchiefs approach to selling art had prevailed. Suddenly feeling tired and limp, I sat down on the sofa, waiting for patrons to arrive.

I dozed off until I heard some activity. The three women I had spoken to the previous night were variously preparing tea, plumping sofa cushions, and greeting an approaching client. The plumper told me this client was their best collector.

I stood and greeted him warmly, expecting to be grilled knowledgeably about techniques and materials. However, he was clearly more interested in attention from the women.

One cheerfully brought him tea while another engaged him in conversation. Her eyes darted in my direction with a clear message: I know how to handle him. You stay out of this.

After a quick look around the room, the man sat down to his tea. I took a chair in the far corner where I could be available if needed. I could hear their conversations.

"Where is this Allan West from?"

"He lives in France."

"These are oil paintings?"

"Yes."

The third woman massaged his shoulders. He hummed contentedly and picked up a sugar cookie. "Hmm ..."

Her fingers kneaded through his shoulder pads. "Aw, c'mon, won't you buy *something?*" she wheedled.

"No, not today. But thanks for the tea."

He left.

Oddly enough, with a name like Allan, some Japanese people assume I'm French, and I don't mind. If I corrected the staff on anything, it would be about the materials I used in a painting and how it was made.

I stopped grinding my teeth long enough to say, "Remember what I told you yesterday about the materials?"

"Oh, they're not oil paintings? But foreigners don't do *nihonga.*"

"Yes, but *I* do."

"Well, I remember you said something about it, but I don't understand art. I was transferred in from ladies' underwear."

Though I was invited to say hello to the occasional patron during the week, I was to sit a safe distance away until the pleasantries were over.

"Customers find it off-putting when artists talk about their work," the women explained. "It gets too technical."

When I remarked how easily the staff acceded to a request to discount a painting, the plumper and the kneader waved off my question, "Oh, he always does that!"

While not permitted to participate myself, I continued to witness conversations—often wildly inaccurate—about me and my work.

This is what a gallery with a *stable* of artists is like from the artist's perspective.

They sold only the paintings I could have sold myself with no effort at all, and I received a fraction of my usual price. This was not at all what I was accustomed to. I might not break even. The materials were expensive, and the process was time consuming. How could I find time to paint at night for exhibitions, twiddle my fingers in the gallery during the day, and still make it work? It was financially impossible.

After the final day of the exhibition ended, I packed up the remaining paintings and received an envelope with the expected financial statement. I had kept a running total in my mind and had a general idea of what the total would be at the bottom.

I opened the envelope and looked closely at each line. After the deductions for tea and cookies, it would barely cover my materials. It became clear that the freely granted discounts were also to

172 · THEY HANG ME IN TOKYO

come from me.

I must have said something under my breath, because the gallery director looked over my shoulder and offered, "Oh, did you break even? I'm so happy for you! That doesn't usually happen."

I worked more hours than the Ministry of Labor workforce legally allows for any employee. If exhibitions like this one were my only source of income, I would have been completely underwater.

It was in the manager's words that I found my future business model. He had said, "I need you in the gallery to sell your art." And that's when I realized I didn't need *him* to sell my art.

I made a decision. A studio of my own could become a dedicated gallery where I could exhibit my art every day of the year. Yet most importantly, I could work while waiting for clients.

It also meant there would be fewer people who would think I was French.

GHOSTS AND OTHER NEIGHBORS

ow that I had decided to sell my work on my own, I needed a studio that would make that possible.

On more than one occasion, people had said, "Tell me the truth: you have a Japanese assistant paint for you, don't you?"

Denying it didn't really help. For that reason, I would need to be situated where passersby could look in and watch me paint. This opportunity to watch the painting's progress provided the perfect proof.

I found an autobody garage that promised to become an excellent art studio. It was in Tokyo's temple district, which has remained virtually unchanged for four hundred years. The light from the north made it ideal. My afternoon was spent clearing rocks from the dirt floor, in preparation for the necessary major renovations.

I took a break to look across the road at the cemetery. People washed gravestones and poured cool water over them to express gratitude to the graves' occupants.

As it is believed the dead progress and develop in stages through-out their afterlife, the survivors purchase from the priest a wooden stake to announce and commemorate each successive stage. Each gravestone is used by a family, and on the back three facets are carved the names of all the individuals whose ashes were interred. Families meet every integer year to have a special meal together, with that person's portrait.

On that first day in the studio, after I had met all my other neigh-bors, I looked out over the graveyard and thought I should greet these sleeping neighbors as well. Hey, everybody, I suppose you get bored at times. Whenever you wish, feel free to stop by.

Our neighborhood, Yanaka, is considered a holy area. Visitors are encouraged to speak in hushed tones, showing respect for the tem-ples and their role of giving spiritual protection to the city.

The rhythm of the neighborhood begins in the early morning when the monks a few doors down gather to chant a sutra. Someone wakes the gods before supplication by ringing a dull-sounding metal *waniguchi*, which resembles an alligator's mouth. Gongs ring out when a parishioner requests a special blessing.

At five in the evening, the deep temple bell rings out the time, and at six o'clock, the rhythmic sutra reading begins. Incense emanates from an unseen source.

My studio blends into this atmosphere, because it now has a three-hundred-year-old facade. It was once part of the Tennoji Temple and later the Kudokurinji Temple. I had been able to rescue the facade just in time before it was destroyed.

We worried about the older men and women who went up and

down the steep incline behind the corner temple. I placed a bench under a canopy of ivy to make a welcoming space in the shade. People rested there after their climb.

A handsome old man named Mr. Kobayashi had been born behind my studio in a small duplex built early in the 20th century. He usually wore tortoiseshell glasses, a dandy hat, and an olive-colored kimono. One day Kobayashi-san offered me a set of zabuton[27] cushions that were almost new, and I gratefully accepted them. I was surprised to learn that he moved to a retirement home the next day.

Next to him was Mrs. Horigome, a woman in her late 80s and one of three widows in our corner. She had a quiet, elegant way about her, and her white hair looked perfect with her simple kimonos. She walked down the hill every day with a wicker shopping basket and greeted me without fail.

A man we knew as *the Kid* lived next door to me, and we shared a wall. He had a workshop in the old barber shop on the other side. I could hear the buzz of his drill press during the late-night hours and into the mornings. He was relieved to know I worked the same hours and didn't mind the sound at all.

This triangle of land had a young couple anchoring the far corner, and my studio held down the other corner. At the most acute corner was the small shop of Saito-san, a woman in her late 70s.

She sold sweets under the broad canopy of the Himalayan cedar tree at the fork in the road. Her store, which was the narrow point of

---

27   The efficient use of living space in Japan means that we sit on the floor. Zabuton cushions help make that easier. With tatami mats on the floor, it doesn't matter how many people one invites, there is always room to sit. Heating is also efficient. When sitting at low tables, they have heaters that warm the legs during the winter. With only that, and a quilted kimono jacket, it is possible to be toasty warm most winter nights.

the triangle, allowed room for only one customer to enter at a time and just enough space for Saito-san to lie down in back with her cat.

All our leases stipulated that we were responsible for repairs and upkeep, and Saito-san continued to repair her small store herself.

BETTER THAN CAKE

A *middle-aged couple had been to my studio a* few times and had bought a print. So, it was fun that they would drop in again on their way home from a pastry shop nearby. It was a famous shop they visited on special occasions.

On this particular day, it was because he had received a transfer that would make a big change in their lives. They were visiting some of their favorite places in Tokyo for perhaps the last time, and I was flattered to learn my studio was on the list of places they would miss.

When she started looking intently at a few of the paintings, I sensed he was a little uncomfortable. He hinted to her about how long they had been walking around and that maybe the parking meter needed to be checked. I realized he didn't want her to get attached to any specific painting.

When she left us briefly, I was wondering how to remove whatever discomfort he was feeling. Then he spoke in a conspiratorial whisper. Their 30th wedding anniversary was coming up soon, and he was hoping to commission a surprise painting for her.

He wanted one that would remind them of fun times together in Tokyo. So, would I please help him discourage her interest in the ones I had out on display? After their morning runs in the park, she loved looking up at the trees in their neighborhood. They were going to miss that park, and he wanted a painting that would remind her of those experiences—perhaps autumn maple leaves and blossoming cherry trees as viewed from below.

He told me the dimensions he wanted. It was to be a surprise, so I must not let on when she came back. When she returned, we were talking about the specifics of his impending transfer. She went back to looking at the paintings and commented on how she liked the mottled effect I had created in silver on one of the backgrounds. I glanced in his direction, and he nodded in a please-take-note-of-that sort of way.

I changed the conversation. "You've seen your new apartment already?"

She turned. "Yes, it will be a little cramped, but the kids are gone now."

I asked if they had decided on a good place for the print they had purchased some years before.

Looking at her, the husband said, "Don't you think it should go in the breakfast nook?"

"Maybe so, but I think something like ..." She started across the room as if to indicate a painting.

The bag she was carrying gave me an excuse to intervene. "Oh, what did you get? Their pound cakes are so incredible."

The husband seized the opportunity to continue diverting her. "We like the cream puffs." To her, he said, "You know, we should have gotten some ice packs for it!" His wife still seemed intent on pointing out a painting she liked, but he said, "I hope our pastries don't melt before we get home."

The thought of ruining their cream puffs was enough, and they said their goodbyes. While he was putting his shoes on, she promised me she would come back before their move, even if it had to be on her own.

The next day, I got an email from his corporate account. He was going to arrange the surprise. I was to use this email address, and if I had any questions, I should feel free to ask.

After I began working on the painting, I got a worried message. The movers were going to pack everything a week before their departure, so the painting needed to be ready earlier than previously arranged. Was that okay?

Sure. It would be close, but I could make it.

I thought of these two and their obviously warm relationship and sense of humor. I imagined them jogging through Yoyogi Park together every evening through all kinds of weather. The branches of the trees intertwined as naturally as I saw their interactions that day in my studio.

They stayed in a distant hotel while the movers were packing everything. The question of how to celebrate came up the day before their anniversary. He had already arranged for me to be on call that day, but he couldn't be sure what time they would arrive. I let him know that everything would be ready and that they could take their time.

That whole day I was on high alert. I started each time I heard the door open. That evening, Mami prepared dinner for our boys, and we waited together in anticipation. It was past closing time, but I had some things to work on and left the lantern on outside.

They drew open the doors.

"How fortunate!" the wife said. "I was sure you'd be closed, but my husband thought we should just peek in the windows even if you were."

He stood behind her at the entrance. "We just bought that cake you recommended, and thought we'd pass by on our way home." He wore a silly grin, and his words sounded rehearsed.

"Well, then," I said, "come on in and have a look around if you like."

They took off their coats and looked slowly from painting to painting. We stood back as they quietly commented to each other on the art. Finally, they came to the end of the wall, and she said, "That's funny. It looks like paper hanging in front of something there. I wonder what that's for."

Her husband took her hand and said, "Let's ask Allan."

I advanced and removed the paper cover.

He said, "It's for you," and she looked at him, not fully understanding. "Happy anniversary. The park, the trees—I had him make this for you."

"It's beautiful! I don't know what to say!" They embraced.

Mami and I made ourselves invisible in the back room, but we could hear happy sounds as they talked quietly about the painting.

After a while, they called after us. We all laughed as she chided us for being in on the secret and not letting on. What great actors we were!

And she could usually figure out what her husband was up to—but not that day!

"I wondered why he thought we should come all this way"—she smiled up at him—"for just a piece of pound cake! Now I know why."

THE FINAL GIFT

mysterious telephone call came as a surprise to Mami. She was unable to place the caller on the other end, though the woman spoke as if they were acquainted.

As the comfortable language of friendship continued, Mami realized the woman felt she knew me because of poring over my website and seeing me interviewed on television.

She was interested in a few of the scrolls she had seen online but was unable to make a final decision. Did I have any more that were not yet on my website?

We sent her a few photographs and suggested that if she had a particular preference for color or motif, I would be more than happy to paint something to fill that need.

She said there wouldn't be time. Mami asked her what her deadline might be and reassured her. If possible, we would arrange the schedule to meet her needs.

The woman hesitated and then poured out her heart. Her father was dying. The hospital had released him because there was nothing more they could do.

She wanted to hang a scroll in the alcove beside his pillow so he could have something beautiful to enjoy during this last stage in his life. There was no way of knowing when that time would come.

The urgency in her voice spoke volumes. Could we mail a scroll or two to them in Yamaguchi for their approval?

We sent a cheerful grouping of flowers and an idealized landscape evocative of a familiar legend. Neither one was exactly right. After a few more tries, I remembered a scroll I had been saving for a unique place, as it was too long to fit in an ordinary alcove.

Painted on gold with silver details in the background, the straight pine tree appeared to be reaching for a place beyond the top of the scroll. The pine appeared to be bathed in bright light, reaching for the sun.

I sent measurements and a photograph. They were delighted. Could I please send it right away?

The scroll just fit, connecting floor and ceiling. Though it might look wrong in the typical alcove, with the roots near the floor, and the crown appearing to extend above the ceiling, the painting drew the eye up from the room and beyond.

Not quite three months later, we received a long letter. The woman said her father had spent his remaining days in and out of consciousness, gazing up at the tree. He had suffered little pain, and he succumbed quietly in his sleep.

WELL-SIDE CONVERSATIONS

It **might seem odd to someone from a** monotheistic culture to learn that when adding the total number of Japanese believers in Shinto with the number who believe in Buddhism, the total is roughly twice the population of Japan.[28]

This is explained by Shinto's animistic understanding of the workings of nature as divine, which gave the ancient Japanese a way to understand disasters. Then later, the arrival of Buddhism during the sixth century CE helped them to deal with the aftermath of disasters stoically.

The uniquely dynamic landscape of Japan is due to its being the only country to sit above two subduction zones while being wedged between four major tectonic plates. This makes volcanoes, earthquakes, and the attendant tsunamis an all-too-common occurrence.

---

28   Edwin O. Reischauer, *The Japanese* (Cambridge: Belknap Press, 1977): 217.

For example, Tokyo has experienced a major earthquake on the average of every 80 years.[29]

In fact, coping with disasters is baked into the cultural fabric in Japan.

There is a reason for the stereotypical walls of paper in a Japanese home. They were a practical way to deal with the uncertainty of life in a dangerous world. Centuries-old scroll paintings depict scattered priests and courtiers carrying sliding-door paintings away from fires, like a trampled colony of ants saving their eggs.

Shrines and temples use such scroll paintings to depict important events in their history. So, invariably, at least one of the scenes deals with some form of disaster. Japanese architecture makes it possible to take apart and reassemble buildings as floodwaters rise or flames advance. This becomes an advantage in a disaster-prone country where brick-and-mortar construction is not as practical or reusable.

Because of standardized units based on the dimensions of tatami floor matting, sliding-door panel paintings can be moved to different buildings without much problem. When the sliding doors need to be retired, for whatever reason, they can be repurposed as folding-screen paintings.

Sometimes they remain as a large suite of hanging scrolls. If you know what to look for, you might find the telltale signs of where a door pull used to be.

The elements bring on both inevitable change and a desire for stability. I was in the alley just behind my studio talking with my neighbor Mr. Kobayashi one day, and Mr. Nitobe,[30] the priest from

---

29 Peter Hadfield, *Sixty Seconds That Will Change the World* (London: Pan MacMillan, 1992): 30-34.

30 The name Nitobe is rare, and one day I asked about it. Mr. Nitobe appeared surprised. Yes, he is in fact related to the noted author of the seminal work *Bushido: The Soul of Japan*, Inazo Nitobe.

the corner temple, came up and joined in. They had long been friends from their days participating in bucket brigade competitions. Preparing for emergencies can also be recreation. Such a conversation as we were having is called a *conference by the well*.

Though Tokyo has provided what is considered modern plumbing as a public service for over four hundred years, many places still maintain a well in case the water main breaks during an earthquake.

In the late '80s, there was a year of regularly occurring earthquakes that had all of us rattled. None of them were strong enough to cause damage, but the frequency was disconcerting.

At one of these impromptu well-side conversations, the idea that perhaps some tectonic plate that had been holding down the progress of another plate had dislodged and allowed this movement to happen was mentioned. Could this be a harbinger of the *big one*?

Another thought was that this was the ideal way for the pressure to be released gradually, rather than all at once—as long as there wasn't any damage. With these constant earthquakes, we were all more than usually aware of emergency exits and whether we had turned off the gas.

The government encouraged everyone to keep a flashlight and a bag of emergency supplies within reach of where we slept. Mami's family offered to store my paintings in their home up north out of the active zone. I took to carrying a backpack with emergency supplies and tools with me whenever I went out.

Eventually, as the earthquakes became weaker and more infrequent, the backpack felt inconveniently heavy, and I returned it to where I slept.

HOW TO SMUGGLE
NOODLES INTO LONDON

O ne day, a couple called Mami to book an appointment at my studio. They had been looking at my paintings online. Seeing my works in person, they claimed to like them even more.

The man was polite and reserved, and he expressed a lot with few words. I learned he was a driven, successful CPA who loved working with his crew. He had enjoyed his years at the Tokyo headquarters of a large financial firm but was to be transferred and would be given responsibility for their London branch.

She was a licensed ikebana instructor, an accomplished cook, and a remarkable interior designer. She found joy in her husband and children. Being a housewife and mother gave her a rich outlet for her creativity.

For him, the transfer was a well-deserved honor, but it meant a lot of change for them and their children. They would miss their Tokyo home and friends. They hoped for a way to take something of Tokyo with them to London—that's where I came in.

I asked them to tell me what they did and didn't like about the artwork on display.

She loved what I could do with oxidizing copper but couldn't rule out the use of patterns in silver or the colors I created out of gold.

"You can't have them all," her husband said. "Why not choose your favorite one?"

I pulled out my brush. "Well, let's see what we can do."

I sketched a backdrop with a silver sky, earth of writhing gold patterns, and a path through it in copper and verdigris. We spent hours around my table at the studio.

I sketched while learning about them. "So, what is it about Tokyo that you'll miss the most?"

"I'll miss my beloved Japanese ikebana plants," she said, "and also being an instructor."

"Oh, and what are some of your favorite plants?"

"I love arranging iris. Also, pine trees and camelias. I'll have to part with my hydrangea bushes and the wisteria arbor out back. I love bamboo and, of course, plum blossoms ..."

Her husband's eyes widened as an apparent signal to stop, but she continued.

"They don't have beautiful maples in London like we have here. I like them when they're fresh and green in the spring. And I can't imagine an autumn without the colors of maple."

Her husband looked worried. "No, that's too much. Allan can't possibly fit all that in."

She wasn't finished. "I like how you paint ferns too. And how could we do without cherry blossoms? I've got to have cherry blossoms."

"It'll ruin the painting," he mumbled.

I began sketching. "Let's see what will work."

With no more than a branch or so of each plant, they all fit, and I was a little surprised. If it worked on this piece of paper, it would be fine on a full-sized folding screen. It would be a challenge, but it looked like a fun project.

I looked across the table at the agitated man who appeared disturbed at the thought of paying for his wife's caprice.

"So," I asked, "what will *you* miss most about Tokyo?"

"My team. My coworkers. We get on really well, and they've made my job a joy."

I wondered how I could possibly express this concept in the painting. He surprised me by adding that his offices were like a warren of busy mice, efficiently scuttering around, neatly going about their jobs. "But, of course, we can't have a mouse in the painting," he said. "That would ruin it."

Clearly, taste and decorum were important to him. I wanted to win him over. After all, this painting was as much his as his wife's.

I asked, "What else will you miss about Tokyo?"

"To be honest, I'll miss my ramen. There's a place I discovered behind the office that is absolutely phenomenal."

His wife pointed to my sketch. "Sorry, but I just can't imagine a bowl of ramen in the middle of this beautiful garden."

I assured them both I did not intend to create an ugly painting.

Mami nodded in agreement.

Her husband looked relieved. "Great. Let me know when you're ready for us to come look at it. And really, don't feel like you need to include all the flowers and everything in there. We'll leave that up to you."

While his wife was talking with Mami, I told him I'd see what I could do about the mouse and the ramen.

"Never mind that. I'll defer to my wife. I'd just rather have her feel pleased with it."

With the sketch as my guide, I started by creating the three bands of metallic leaf for the base. This would be the armature onto which the plants would be added. To prevent uneven drying, I must lay down the leaf all at one session.

This meant preparing all the food I would need for the two-day marathon—plenty of Calorie Mate and pistachios. I needed to think like a machine; the more regular my motions became, the fewer mistakes. I could only take breaths once the gold leaf was applied and before I took out the next one. Any hurried motion may have caused the gold leaf to break apart. I listened to radio dramas to keep me awake.

The branches came next, each claiming their territory. So much depended on the branches that this took the most concentration. I needed total silence. Once the branches were set, I filled in the leaves of each plant, careful that none were squeezed out.

The weeks of painting leaves could become tedious. I listened to dramas so that I never needed to take my eye from my work.

The flowers came next. This was the most fun part. I listened to Boccherini. With the addition of the flowers, the whole painting came to life. They obscured much of the work I had done with the branches and leaves. I didn't begrudge this because this was just like what we see in nature. Flowers blossomed in front of the rest of the plant. The position of the flower depended on the branch. And without the branch behind, there would be no way to determine the flower's natural location.

When at last the painting was complete, the couple arrived. I offered them a seat and opened the screen. The moment had come to hand it over.

My paint and brush were ready. And, subject to their approval, I would add my signature in their presence.

Getting the multiplicity of colors to harmonize had been the most challenging part of the painting, but I was satisfied with it. The intertwining branches and leaves were pleasing, and the three horizontal areas of metallic leaf provided unity.

The man watched the gold leaf capture the glow from the window and asked, "How does it do that? This is fantastic, thank you!" Clearly relieved, he said, "To be honest, this is better than I expected."

His wife chimed in, "Well, I knew it would be good."

We discussed the techniques, and the man and woman were both surprised all the plants and flowers had been included. I pointed out the place for my signature. Just above it, in vermilion, was a small mouse climbing on a gourd, painted to appear as a signature seal.

The gourd is a symbol of prosperity and good luck. Paired with the mouse, it also suggests the Shinto deity *Daikoku*, who brings wealth. It seemed like the right symbol for the man's new assignment.

I got the tissue papers to protect the folds and pack the painting in its case. As the new owner, the man came over to supervise the process.

While we worked, I stealthily showed him a cupped blossom with stamens in gold. The stamens in that one particular cup formed a remarkably wavy pattern. They could almost be mistaken for some kind of, dare I say, *noodle-like substance?*

With the folding screen in its case, it was ready for its journey to London as the newest addition to their family.

The woman said, "I'm glad you've included something in the painting for my husband. Thank you. What a clever way to include the mouse, but I'm glad you decided not to paint any ramen!"

Her words elicited a chuckle from her husband, and he glanced my way. Though brief and private, his reaction was meaningful and gave me a singular satisfaction.

I loved having Mami involved in this experience—and knowing she enjoyed being at the studio.

My muse had returned.

FILLING MY TOOLBOX

One evening, my son Ray came to the dinner table with a book in his hand. "Guess what, Dad—this story could be about you! I mean, this guy Mokichi did exactly what you've been doing."

He handed me the book—volume seven of *Gintama* by Hideaki Sorachi. Beginning from the place where he held his thumb I read a story that I remember going something like this:

During the Edo period,[31] there was a story about two well-known carpenters. One was Gohei, the son of a wealthy family. Not only was his ability as a craftsman excellent, but he also knew how to use his position of privilege to get ahead.

The other carpenter, Mokichi, was considered a strange sort, who

---

31   The period is named for Edo, the de facto capital of Japan from 1603 until 1868, at which time governing powers were returned to the emperor, and the city became the official capital and was renamed Tokyo. Andrew Gordon, *A Modern History of Japan* (New York: Oxford University, 2003).

cared little for fame or fortune. His carpentry work was his happiness. Wielding his hammer gave him more joy than food or drink.

As the story continued, Gohei wanted to be considered the foremost carpenter in the entire capitol city of Edo. He used his influence to make sure all the easiest, most prestigious, well-paying jobs came to himself. He also made certain the most complicated, unreasonable, and difficult projects were passed on to Mokichi.

I continued to read with interest. Mokichi's reputation plummeted when people saw that the projects he was awarded were less important and more difficult. They wondered about his abilities as a carpenter.

While he accepted one seemingly impossible or challenging situation after another, Mokichi's career suffered and stalled.

As it did, Gohei succeeded. Before long, Gohei was indeed considered the most influential and respected carpenter in all of Edo.

But the story does not end here.

Over time, Mokichi's reputation began to surge. In fact, it rose until it overtook that of Gohei. How could that have happened despite all Gohei's clever plans?

Curious about the reason for Mokichi's success, Gohei went to Mokichi and asked, "You haven't done anything devious to succeed, now have you? I know you have been forced to undertake some truly dreadful projects. I expected you to concede defeat."

"That is just the thing," Mokichi replied. "It is true I have been given some great challenges. Each one has pushed me to sharpen my skills and improve my technique. Difficult conditions forced me to be resourceful—to invent new ways of solving problems, and I'm a better carpenter for it."[32]

To my surprise, Ray had known of my struggles. With each difficult job, I had added a new tool to my skillset. As I walked to the studio that night, I felt deeply gratified to know my son understood.

32　空知英秋，銀魂，第7巻（東京：集英社，2005): 101-2. My translation.

THE SMITHSONIAN

Washington, *DC, attorney and art collector Daniel Q. Callister* was especially enthusiastic about my art. The large painting he commissioned for his hallway was what had made it possible for me to move to Tokyo years before. I believe it was on visiting his home that the director of the Smithsonian's Renwick Gallery, Elizabeth Broun, was first introduced to my work.

Late one night as I was painting, the silence of my studio was broken by the telephone. A fax from the secretary of the Renwick Gallery had sent me an invitation to bring some art to show the curator.

I had a folding-screen painting in Washington, DC. So the next time I was in town, I made an appointment, and I took that painting to show her. She was impressed and asked me all about it, quizzing me about specific color choices and motifs.

I had learned that people often asked these questions when

the painting didn't communicate. I feared the work was a failure. Shouldn't a great painting answer its own questions?

I believe that if onlookers need additional information to enjoy a painting, something is not right. The painting should be able to reveal itself gradually, and continued contact should maintain interest. It should be able to stand on its own.

At the end of our meeting, Elizabeth Broun said, "Don't be so self-effacing about your work. I love what you're doing. I want to see how it might fit into our schedule." She added, "But an artist needs to be able to talk about his work, and I shouldn't have to draw it out of you."

I had received no commitment, but she seemed positive. This was more than I had expected, and that alone was reason to rejoice.

She probably saw the excitement on my face and wanted to bring me down easily. So, as we were leaving, she made a point of saying, "This isn't going to make your career. Nothing's going to change."

As we pushed open the heavy doors to leave, Dan's eyes widened, and I mouthed, "Wow!"

SUITABLE

After returning to Japan, I eventually received confirmation from the Smithsonian and attacked my preparations for the exhibition with enthusiasm. While I was hard at work, a friend dropped by to say he had seen my suite of sliding-door panels for a temple in Tokyo while attending a funeral the previous night.

I asked, "Oh, did someone tell you I painted it?"

He said, "No. But they didn't need to. The painting was so obviously yours."

I felt a swell of pride to hear from him that my artwork was easily recognizable.

Late that night, I received a disappointing fax from the Smithsonian. Because I was an American, they could only requisition funds to transport the artwork from within the United States. I would have to find another way to arrange for the shipping costs from Japan.

I couldn't let this opportunity escape me, but I had no idea where to turn. Like my parents sometimes said, there's many a slip between the cup and the lip. It had often proved to be true. The more delays and complications that arose in any project, the greater likelihood of failure. I would have to be vigilant.

How should I approach people for assistance in shipping my artwork for this exhibition? And what should I wear to this kind of meeting? That was the kind of question Dad would ask to help me prepare.

When I moved to Japan, his question had changed to "Who was there, and what were you wearing?" He wanted to be sure I made a good impression.

It took me some time to develop a style that left a mark and spoke clearly of *my* profession—not that of a lawyer.

———

The incident that caused me to rethink my style happened one evening while I was at a networking reception. Whenever I was asked which *firm* I worked for, I presented my card.

Allan West, nihonga artist.

They looked at me in my suit, then back at the card with confusion, if not derision or distaste.

I had to change the impression I made. So I stopped wearing the suits I didn't feel I had the right to wear and instead wore traditional Japanese clothing, but with my own permutations.

I wore a Zen priest's shirt but with craftsman's pants. Over that I wore the sleeveless jacket of a person committed to the arts. Under my shirt, I wore a collar as one would do for formal kimonos. A necktie pin kept the collar shut. On my feet were *tabi* socks and black-lacquer clogs. The collar correlated with the necktie, the jacket with the suit coat, and so on. Even the lacquer clogs evoked well-shined leather shoes.

This combination is uniquely mine, but to the Japanese, it suggests someone who is dedicated to the arts, understands traditional culture, and is comfortable with formality. I have arrived at this after a 20-year period of trial and error. It is practical and works well for me.

My father had difficulty understanding and even accepting what I wore—but it was essential that I dress like a nihonga painter, put my clients at ease, and do my job.

Now when I present my name card, I'm greeted with "I knew you did something of the sort. So that's what it is!" My clothing prepares potential clients in advance.

My father and I have had our ups and downs. And at times, Japan didn't seem far enough away. I might be excited and energized by one telephone call, but then there were other calls that left me drained.

This is my life, and I'm going to live it my way would circulate through my head for days. Subtle things he said would eat at me. They were unintentionally and unconsciously expressed reminders of his toleration.

My mother would say, "Steve was excited to tell the neighbors all about your new project!"

I appreciated those glimpses, but they didn't come directly from him.

There were times I wanted or needed to hear an apology, but I never got one. More recently, I heard him speak of times when it might seem proper for a corporation to apologize. He said, however, in court, an apology could be taken as an admission of guilt and would leave the corporation open to litigation.

I understood the point but still thought the effort toward making amends was what an apology should be all about.

I had art teachers who were miserly in their praise. They knew that we would be particularly motivated by the scarcity of it. Sometimes I even saw through that tactic. But if it was a conscious tactic in my father, I couldn't see through it.

53

DISSING YOKO ONO

I *did an interview with the in-flight magazine for* a Japanese airline, and it was well received. It happened just a few years after the fall of the Berlin Wall, when wall debris was still evident, and Berlin was still bisected.

The airline had its ticketing office in the center of West Berlin, on a fashionable corner of the Europa Center—an enclave of upscale boutiques. Their building had an expanse of open windows facing the plaza. The area had once been the gathering place for bohemian and intellectual culture.

The airline chose to use this office as gallery space to add culture to their image. They invited me to exhibit there.

I was encouraged to enjoy the city but also to stay in the gallery if I could—to answer any questions a patron might have.

The airlines had three ticketing agents there to protect the artwork, but beyond that, more active efforts on behalf of the exhibition would have to be mine. I solicited cafés to hang my posters. The next day, I sat for a while but got so eager to visit the Pergamon Museum that I left.

When I got back from the museum and East Berlin, an animated agent said, "While you were gone, the best-selling author Tamba Tetsuro came! We did what we could to answer his questions. When they ask what a painting *means*," she shrugged, "what should we say?"

I felt a painting should not be tied down to a meaning, so it could be open to the viewer's interpretation, like music. The question of how invested I should be in abstraction was an ongoing issue for me. Still, I was sorry she had felt on the spot.

"I wish I had an easy answer for you," I said, "but I don't want to impose my intentions on anyone."

I saw artwork as a form of collaboration; it's not complete until it has been seen and experienced. Until then, it is like a letter—delivered but still unopened.

I stayed with the exhibit the next day to take questions myself, but almost no one came.

The next day, *Der Tagesspiegel* gave me a glowing review entitled "Farbstrudel."

What on earth did my artwork have to do with pastries? My friend translated *Farbstrudel* for me. It meant "whirlpools of color."

After getting the complete translation, I went to an opera. Upon my return, the three excited attendants told me that Kayama Yūzō, Japan's Frank Sinatra, had come. He had left just moments ago.

After such excitement, I felt obligated to stay until closing. Though many people stopped and looked at the artwork through the windows, not a single person came in. But next morning, I decided. After all the fun I had had in Berlin, I really needed to show the staff I was serious about the exhibition. So, I stayed.

An elderly woman walked in and looked at each painting. But she spent an unusually long time in front of one in particular.

It was a cheerful, airy scroll painting of clouds and shafts of light that I had done with *sumi* ink on white paper. I tried to be as inconspicuous as possible as I watched her.

I was touched as she approached me with wet eyes. She said the painting brought back an experience she had in the Second World War, a painful experience. It brought to her mind the memory of watching a house blow up across the street!

I was surprised and disappointed—but glad she had confided this to me.

My ability to communicate through my art was not as I had thought. Had I painted more concrete information, maybe it wouldn't have stimulated these unpleasant memories in her.

What use is abstraction if, instead of expressing the boiled-down essence of a thing, it just becomes a cipher? I had wanted to leave the information in a painting open to the viewer for free exploration, but how specific should I be? I want to allow viewers to connect with a painting on their own terms. Ideally, the viewer and I should meet halfway.

I thanked the woman for her story. The questions it raised in me may never be resolved, but I return to them even now.

I appreciated the attendants pressing me to get lunch. I needed to think. At a nearby café, I stared into space. How necessary was abstraction to a painting? In communicating the essence of a work, how important was it to portray things as they appear?

The balance between abstract and figurative may tip, occurring earlier or later in the painting process. When a painting appears to be finished, I have to stop.

Still deep in thought, I returned to the gallery and saw all three women standing at the door waiting for me. In chorus, they exclaimed, "You just passed her! Why didn't you say something? That was Yoko Ono. She came to change her reservations. We tried to keep her here until you came back."

I had been too deep in thought and missed yet another notable guest. But that was all right. I learned a lot about art and communication in Berlin. This question of mine may never be fully settled. But my attitude toward the viewer and what I want them to see in my art had changed.

After all my musings and indecision, I had come to understand one thing: if art signifies nothing, it can signify anything. If it can signify anything, it signifies nothing.

54

IDENTITY MATTERS

As a result of my exhibit with the Japanese airlines in Berlin, I was emboldened to approach the airline's cultural affairs department. Might they help me ship the artwork to the United States for my Smithsonian exhibition?

As they wished to present an image of high culture and Japanese hospitality, the airline decided to do so. But this was only if I could arrange to give them recognition for their services on the wall text and in printed materials at the museum. I told them I would find out if that was possible.

When I contacted the Smithsonian, I received a guarded response. At that time, most museums were not yet as cautious about being used by disreputable corporations trying to improve their public image. This airline was different. The Smithsonian decided it was possible to meet that request but with some restrictions. With that, I felt the last impediment to the exhibition had been cleared. I was going to have to send photographs for approval soon.

Front-page news in Japan is usually about foreign politics and occurrences. It would not be unusual for a Japanese person to know who the American president is but not who Japan's current prime minister might be.

People born in the 1960s are perhaps the last to continue certain customs in significant numbers—to sleep in futons on the floor covered by reed tatami mats and to eat sitting on the floor at a low table. Most now sleep in a Western bed, sit on chairs at a table for dinner, and have taken etiquette lessons at school on how to use a knife, fork, and spoon.

The children my generation gave birth to were raised in a completely Western style. Most have never walked on a tatami mat, slept on a futon, or worn a kimono.

But there is an interesting change occurring. It is exactly because of this infusion of Western culture that Japanese young people now see their native culture as exotic. Though putting on a formal kimono is complicated and daunting, during the summer fireworks display, a casual form of the kimono is now considered almost necessary.

During my student years, Naito-san was a studious fellow who lived halfway down the hall from me in the boardinghouse. He wore round glasses over his smiling eyes and was studying at Tokyo University while I was still preparing for my entrance examinations. We had some interesting debates about politics and culture, and he showed an interest in my perspective.

Naito-san made an interesting request.

He said that his contact with the most traditional aspects of Japanese historical culture often made him feel like a foreigner in his own country, whereas I seemed entirely comfortable with Japan's traditional culture. Would I be willing to visit the Tokyo National Museum with him and answer his questions about the art collection there?

It was a surprising request—mostly because I hadn't fully under-

208 · THEY HANG ME IN TOKYO

stood the distance Japanese people of our generation felt from their own native culture.

The visit was remarkable. Naito-san's keen intellect was evident in his probing and stimulating questions. I expected nothing less from a student at Tokyo University. His desire to understand applied to this museum outing as well.

Naito-san had been accepted to Columbia University, and he wanted to prepare for questions from his fellow students about the culture of his native country. I had provided the crash course in Japanese art.

Not long after that, a new discovery was made in South Africa. It changed my perspective on the painting technique I thought I had invented. Yes, I had come to acknowledge that the Japanese had me beat by a couple of millennia, and I was grateful that not only were some people still working in that medium but that, by refinement over the ages, the materials and tools in Japan had improved.

In the caves of the Blombos region of South Africa, there was discovered in 2008 not only the world's oldest known cave painting but beside it another cave archaeologists call *the paint factory.*

Approximately a hundred thousand years ago, the making of paint for the cave had been abruptly abandoned in midprocess. The materials and tools were all there to see. This was a huge discovery, because until that point, the materials and techniques used for cave paintings had been the subject of speculation. As an elementary school kid, I had been taught that the paints were thought to have been made from dirt mixed with pine pitch. We now know from the evidence in the Blombos caves that the hides of the now-extinct aurochs had been rendered for protein. Red ocher and yellow ocher stones were pulverized by a large boulder that would have taken three men to raise.

Ocher and protein were combined in abalone shell bowls. To this day, fingerprints of the prehistoric paint maker remain on the shell where the paint was blended by hand.

These innovators had rolled the mixture of mineral dust and animal protein to make sticks, a kind of primitive pastel. This was truly one of the oldest forms of human expression to have been discovered,[33] and the materials and methods were the same as those now used for nihonga.

We have the Japanese to thank for continuing the use of this most ancient of techniques and for raising it to its present level. We see in Blombos that this heritage actually belongs to all humankind.

Without fully understanding what I had done, my experiments had taken me across the world and then back to another era—from modern to prehistoric times. In Japan, I had found the painting materials that were right for me, as I had long strived to do.

---

33   C.S. Henshilwood, J.C. Sealy, and R. Yates, "Blombos Cave, Southern Cape, South Africa: Preliminary Report on the 1992–1999 Excavations of the Middle Stone Age Levels," *Journal of Archaeological Science* 28, no. 4 (2001): 421–48.

55

MY TALL FRIEND

We human beings have a remarkable ability to connect emotionally with plant life. Bouquets are entrusted with conveying our sincerest feelings. We have a long tradition of bringing plants indoors to brighten bleak winters. Plant motifs dominate the clothing we wear and patterns on our walls and floors.

As an artist who grew up in the Christian tradition, I often think of the creation and hold the belief that, in some premortal form, we may have been present to witness it. I am in awe to think of the sacredness imbued in a tree by that divine act and will always hope to express echoes of that event in my work. But imbuing spiritual properties in a tree is not easy for a mere painting to do. During our lifetimes, perhaps a tree is as close as we can expect to come to what the divine has left for us in nature.

In Japan, we acknowledge the significance of trees in our lives in various ways. In one of the nine scrolls I painted for the Shuvalov Palace, a maple branch has a bell to attract heavenly notice. In another, a protective amulet is tied to a wisteria branch to strengthen its effect. A ginkgo tree has a pile of pebbles in the crook of a branch in memory of those who have passed on. A straw rope, used to indicate the boundaries of the holiest precincts, encircles a cedar tree.

A fortune-telling strip is tied to a plum branch to make sure it will come true. Lightning-shaped paper strips are hung from the trunk of a willow tree as a sign of Shinto purification. An *ema* prayer plaque hangs from a cherry tree.

In legend, Noh drama[34] and Kabuki,[35] the spirit of plants and animals, often appear in human form to instruct us to be more selfless, to enjoy the beauties of nature, or to rejoice. This attitude has its roots in Shinto animism.

I chose the location of my studio in part because of the glorious spreading Himalayan cedar on the corner. I sensed it had always been there and that it always would be. It was comforting to think it would one day see my death and continue on. This tree was considered the *nushi* of the neighborhood.

The word *nushi* has many connotations. It suggests a wise, respected, and aged protective presence. I can hear its breath with the wind in its branches. When turning the corner on the way home, I would see the cedar waiting at the end of the block as if to welcome me.

---

34 Noh came together as a dramatic form in the 14th century, although many of its elements are much older. The main character is usually masked. The subject matter is mainly legendary figures and their dealings with the spiritual realm. The slow, ritualized movements and music are intended to put the viewer into a trancelike state. Faubion Bowers, *Japanese Theatre* (Rutland, VT: Charles E. Tuttle Company, 1974).

35 Kabuki originated in the 17th century as a dramatic form that appealed to the masses. It uses exaggerated makeup, costumes, and actions to portray recent scandals or obliquely critical reference to governing powers. Bowers, *Japanese Theatre*.

"The mountains and the hills shall break forth before you into singing, and all the trees of the field shall clap their hands" (Isaiah 55:12) KJV.

Over the decades I have spent in the cedar's shade, I have seen its branches extend over the wall of the graveyard across the street. The five trunks that fork out about eight feet above the ground create an awning over the three roads that connect Yanaka.

Myogyoji Temple, Zuirinji Temple, the corner sweetshop of Saito-san, and Abe-san's house next door are covered by this canopy. Saito-san's sweetshop is named for these three corners. In addition to the inexpensive treats children can buy with a few yen, she sells postcards of the tree and tree-shaped cookies. People come from far away just to visit this beloved tree.

Saito-san's rusted tin roof collects the needles inches deep. Once when I offered to sweep them off before the rain made them heavier, she said, "It doesn't matter. The rain doesn't get through the tree anyway."

STILL WAITING[36]

There is an ancient Japanese tradition that explains the origin of the arts: Long, long ago, in the time of legends, humankind and the gods lived together in a village not far away. At the end of work each day, they would gather and rest at the center square, beneath the spreading branches of the tallest tree. There they learned from the gods how to live with love, do right by their fellow men, and fulfill their potential as part of the village community. This was a happy time, and they lived in harmony.

One evening, as the villagers gathered in the town square, the gods announced they had an errand to run but would soon return. With that, they disappeared up the old tree and into the heavens. The villagers watched under the tree and waited until late in the night, but the gods did not return.

---

36   Adapted from my TEDx talk.

Days passed, and they feared the details of what they had learned from the gods might be forgotten. Time grew heavy. As they reminisced about all the lessons they had learned, one person told of the ideas in a narrative form, and the first story was born. Another put the story to music, creating the first song. Other villagers invented art and literature to record them.

The villagers revered the old tree that had transported the gods to heaven, and they named the pine tree *Matsu*—the waiting tree, or *Matsu no ki*. Remembering how they felt in the presence of the gods, they considered the tree and the clearing in front a holy place.

From that time forward, Japan's traditional performing arts have taken place before the image of an aged and venerable waiting tree of pine. It is believed such trees bind heaven and earth and that such a backdrop serves to welcome the gods' return and encourage their participation.

Vestiges of this legend continue in the arts. The backdrop of a Noh drama must have a painting of an old pine; the stage itself represents the clearing. Even now, the Noh stage is considered a sacred space, and anyone walking on it is required to wear *tabi* socks out of respect. So, when there is not a specific stage set for *Nihon-buyō* dancing or Kabuki, the ancient-pine motif is used as a backdrop.

I once saw a newly built Noh theater stage that had a painting of little pine seedlings covering the back wall. The actors did not approve. The artist and local government that built the theater hadn't known the legend.

What is lost when the legend is forgotten?

The aim of modernism has come to destroy the previous social functions of art and aesthetics. It rejects the usefulness of beauty, history, wisdom of the ages, and our connections to nature. It belittles faith, discipline, and tradition—all the things so important to health, the human heart, society, and a vital culture. These are the very things that mattered most to the legendary villagers.

At one time, there was a logical reason for modernism. It freed us from the tight strictures of academia. But modernism had its limitations. Now it has outlived this original purpose. The values modernism embraced in the beginning have now become toxic.

Generally, modernists are not concerned with what effect their art has on people, and because of that, they often deliberately avoid having any message at all.

They may disorient the viewer by changing the size, makeup, or context of a mundane object. It's not as much about what is being said as *how* it is being said.

Even so, it's natural for people to read meaning into the artwork; that's just what we do. And so, the by-product of this natural desire for meaning is that a totally unintended message is associated with the artwork in unpredictable ways.

Some modernists send a message to invoke strong emotional reactions, such as disgust, anger, or horror, to get attention.

The ideal is to have the greatest impact using the simplest of means.

About a decade ago, while considering these modernistic ideals, I wondered what could possibly serve as the ultimate example of the modernistic approach toward expression.

One single work that I could not erase from my mind exemplifies what modernism has become in its purest form. It was not intended to be art, but nevertheless, through the lens of modernism, it was one powerful, site-specific performance piece.

That one event was 9/11.

Shock.

It fits all the criteria. It challenged our perceptions on an enormous scale. This one thing had the greatest emotional impact.

We artists have developed standards that are so toxic and unrelated to responsibility that such an act of terror meets and exceeds modernism's ideal artistic criteria. Where will we go from here?

57

ALL THINGS MUST DISAPPEAR

I was chosen to paint the sliding-door panels for the main sanctuary of the Kamidaigo-ji Temple, high on the mountain peak. This temple was more than a thousand years old.

Months earlier, I had held an exhibition at the museum of the temple, and they'd liked what they'd seen.

Nervous with excitement, I passed through the gated gardens of the expansive temple complex below. The early-morning mist still obscured the top of the mountain. I was coming for an important meeting to learn the details of their proposal.

An agitated monk led me to the conference room. "Did you see the news?" he asked.

I had not. He left me. I waited—and waited some more. Several apologies later, the abbot entered to explain the delay: lightning had struck the mountaintop temple. The ensuing fire had destroyed it completely.

He shook his head. "A great national treasure is lost. But the holy words of our Old Ajari will heal the sorrow. When we carried him up to see the destruction, he said, 'All things that have form must eventually disappear.'"

These words of Old Ajari point to the folly of becoming attached to physical things. But they also help me remember the intangible things I most value.

Year by year, the number of nihonga painters is decreasing, and with them go the livelihoods of many people who are indispensable to our work. The craftspeople who create the materials I need are gradually dying out. I have nothing but gratitude for them.

A few years ago, I was in Kanazawa, the city of workshops where gold leaf is made. I wanted to thank the man who beats the gold leaf I buy. I entered a thickly padded room with a large and noisy hydraulic stamper. The man was moving a package of gold foil under the blur of the machine's bit, when I noticed two of his finger joints were missing. I learned this was a common accident for goldbeaters. Until then I hadn't fully understood the sacrifice made by these craftspeople.

Years ago, I was applying gold leaf to a pair of folding screens. In a new package of gold leaf, there was a hole or a tear in almost every other sheet. I was able to patch them, so it wasn't a problem. But it took away valuable time.

The next time I went to buy gold leaf from that vendor, he apologized for the defects. It seemed the master beater had passed away unexpectedly, and his apprentice had not yet completed his training. "But let's give him a few more months," the vendor said. As my project continued, the gold leaf had fewer imperfections and I found myself cheering for this distant unseen person. Wow, that was 10 perfect ones in a row!

From that time, I have imagined the person behind each of the items I've used.

Licia is the name we use in Japanese for a special dark-green pigment I paint with most of the time. Using green as much as I do, I need to have it consistently available.

Ten years ago, I was working on a painting of a bamboo grove and needed a large packet of licia. After searching in the back of her shop, Matsushita-san gave me what little she could find. She said the seam had been completely mined out. I would have to do without until they could discover another one.

All that year, the situation was tense.

Another vein was discovered farther north, but our good fortune was to end later with the Tōhoku earthquake. This new seam of licia was now off-limits because it was within the newly established Fukushima nuclear reactor exclusionary zone.

My own jars of pigment had survived, and the pigment store had minimal damage from the quake, but the licia could last only so long. I would have to wait another year for a new vein to be found.

The linchpin for the whole process of painting is *nikawa*. This animal-protein glue is what turns the powdered pigments into paint. Without nikawa, there is no painting. Even ink requires this deer-bone protein.

Nikawa sticks are like glass rods. I wrap them in a towel to protect my hands from shards while I snap them down to a workable size. Then I heat them in a double boiler until they melt.

I use shells for containers,[37] as the Blombos cave dwellers did a hundred thousand years ago—and as the Kano school masters did in the Edo period. The shell transfers the heat of my hand, keeping the protein warm and liquid.

The protein retains the properties it had when it was alive. We were taught to treat it as a living thing. Heated too quickly, its adhesive strength diminishes. Cold water makes it shrink. And during the summer, the nikawa might sour.

For a long time, there was only one workshop making this protein glue. I heard through the grapevine that the business was not doing well. The president of the University of the Arts, one of the influential Five Mountains, had done a lot to encourage the family to stay in business. Then the president died, and their motivation to keep up production disappeared.

I stockpiled enough for a year, but after all the stores were sold out, I worried that there would be no more. I scoured the shops for the amber-colored sticks and alerted my friend, a junk shop owner, to look out for them. But furniture makers were desperate for the adhesive nikawa as well.

About this same time, I got bad news from my friend Yokoo-san and the mounters at his company, Masumi. The weavers who supplied as much as a third of the silks I used to mount my scrolls were now defunct.

Their business had been not so much a company as a complex system. The weavers hired loom threaders, thread dyers, and pattern designers. The thread dyers depend on thread twiners and dye

---

37   Though the Blombos cave dwellers used abalone, I use shells of the surf clam because they fit into my hand perfectly.

makers, and on and on. The network of people necessary for such a business was staggering. It took centuries to develop such a complicated symbiotic relationship. It would be impossible now to bring together a new one. The only option we had left was to hold on tight to what there was.[38]

I was bereft. My options as an artist were gradually closing in. How much longer might I enjoy this hard—won freedom?

Not long after that, a division of a food-processing company started making nikawa in a subdivision of its gelatin plant. They made it according to the food-safety standards of the Ministry of Health and Welfare. For purposes of painting, it was awful. But after a few months of their tweaking the process, acceptable nikawa was once again available. For now, I try to be encouraged by whatever is back to normal.

Each generation has had its own ordeals. My professor Kayama[39] sensei spoke of when he was a student at Tokyo University of the Arts during World War II. Nikawa was in great demand.

Because metals were scarce, there were no nails. Airplanes were made with canvas stretched over wooden frames,[40] and the canvas was glued down with nikawa.

One artist, an alumnus, had an uncle in the military. This uncle requisitioned just enough of the precious glue for his alma mater, so my professor and his fellow students at the Tokyo University of the Arts were able to continue painting.

38 My dependence on Yokoo-san and the expert mounters at his company further extend this complex codependent relationship.
39 Professor Kayama was particularly short and slight, and I suspect that the privations he suffered during the war at that age had something to do with it.
40 This type of plane was called 赤蜻蛉 (Red Dragonfly) and白菊 (White Chrysanthemum), and they were evidence of the resourcefulness of the Japanese military during extreme privation.

This was the only arts university in Japan considered important enough to keep open during the war. Rather than risk being sent to the front lines, Japan's most talented students were allowed to attend there and study traditional painting as a way to preserve their culture.

Kayama sensei was one of the recipients of a meager portion of this glue. As a student, he was not allowed any meat for weeks at a time because of food rationing. He said nikawa could be quite tasty, and he was tempted to drink the pure protein mixture.[41]

One student could not resist and did drink his nikawa and, because of that, could not complete the project he was painting. He was therefore unable to remain a student and was sent to war, where he later died.

As I heat the nikawa over my charcoal brazier and watch the steam rise, I think of the sacrifices people have made and of the trials nihonga artists have endured in the past.

Nihonga is treasured today, yet at the same time, endangered. Though it is called nihonga now, this same technique, seen in cave paintings, once belonged to all humankind.

With the beginning of oil paints during the Renaissance, the West gradually forgot this foundational technique. It now remains mostly in Japan; however, Japan, too, is beginning to forget. Mass-produced oil paints are cheaper and simple to use. As people become more impatient and less discerning, I wonder whether nihonga can compete.

One day a sad thought came to me: This may be the best it gets.

---

41 In order to prepare nikawa for the sizing undercoat, alum must be added. In class, Kayama sensei showed us how, as we gradually add alum to the protein broth, the proper proportions are reached when the mixture becomes tasty. I think of this every time I dip my finger in to test my sizing.

I will do all I can to keep it alive for as long as possible, until the materials I need are no longer available—then I will be able to look back and know I did all I could.

I'm grateful for each day it is possible to continue.

58

MISSION IMPROBABLE

ach collaboration with a client is an adventure. Some more so than others.

For years, I greeted Dante and his wife, Setsuko, as they walked past my studio. One day they stepped inside and wanted to see everything I had.

I mentioned it was a shame I was missing the paintings I had sent to Amsterdam for an exhibition three years ago. They still hadn't been returned to me.

I told Dante and Setsuko how the gallery owner had dealt with my attempts to reach him. He met some of my calls with placating responses. After a while, he became evasive.

Then, after that, he no longer answered my calls. I left recorded messages—still no response. My faxes, emails, and letters were also ignored.

Not one of my messages was accusatory. I wanted only to know what his plans were for the 20 or so paintings I had sent to him. Had they sold? Were they still on display?

When I told Dante of the situation, he wondered if the gallery had gone out of business.

The blood drained from my face.

The painting Dante and Setsuko planned to commission was to be for their home in Europe. Would I consider visiting them there? It might be helpful if I could see the place in their living room where they intended to hang it.

But they were curious about what was in Amsterdam and made an interesting proposal: on my trip, we should go and rescue the paintings being held hostage there.

My imagination raced. Had the paintings been scattered to the four corners? I had a friend whose paintings were considered an asset of a gallery that filed for bankruptcy, so he never did get them back.

At Dante and Setsuko's home, they rolled out the red carpet for me. I was excited to be part of their dinner party and to enjoy their beautiful city. I sketched scenes from their garden as inspiration for the folding screen that would go in their living room.

Dante thought I should rescue the orphaned paintings as soon as possible. I didn't fly all the way to Europe just to return empty handed. So, he rented a truck, and we set off early the next morning for Amsterdam.

Dante was a chemist who had also studied law. He would make sure everything was on the up and up. But while on the ride, we imagined many risky and disastrous scenarios, and the theme song from *Mission Impossible* played over and over in my head.

We found the gallery on its street corner and parked the truck. This was going to be an unexpectedly realistic stakeout. We even had the necessary jelly doughnuts.

I went up to check the front door. It was locked, and the lights were off. I feared my worst nightmares had come true. The gallery appeared to have gone out of business.

Then Dante pointed to the sign on the door. The posted business hours indicated it wouldn't open for another 20 minutes—if it even opened at all.

We moved the truck to a better vantage point across from the gallery to watch and wait.

I had borrowed a pair of mother-of-pearl opera glasses because there were no binoculars. The opera glasses were less bulky anyway.

The time for the gallery to open had come and gone. How much longer would we have to wait? A lanky figure with platinum-blond hair turned the corner.

It was our man.

We watched him fiddle with his keys, drop them, and finally open the door. I adjusted my cap to a cunning angle. We walked briskly enough to keep him in sight, but not so fast as to be noticed. He flipped the sign over to show he was open.

Leaving the front door open, he made his way to the rear and switched on the lights in the back room. The gallery was still dark.

I crept between boxes and crates to the office door and blocked it with my arms on each of the jambs. Dante filled the front door with his body to provide further protection and prevent the man's escape. I hoped there was no rear exit.

The gallery owner looked up and saw me at the office entrance. Occupied with making myself look big and impressive, I cleared my throat, hoping to make my voice lower and more intimidating.

"Allan! You surprised me."

"Really?" I squeaked.

"What are you doing here?"

"Um ... uh."

"You should have told me you were coming!"

Just then the phone rang. He picked up the receiver and replaced it quickly.

"Actually," I said, "I've been trying to contact you for over a year, but you never answered my faxes and emails."

The phone rang again. The caller received the same treatment I had experienced.

"I'll let the machine take the message," he said.

The answering machine clicked on with the familiar words. "Please leave your name and number ..."

"Hello? This is the attorney from—"

He picked up the receiver quickly and, putting his hand to his mouth, said, "I'm in an important meeting right now. Let me call you back."

I could hear a voice on the other end protesting as he hung up the phone. As soon as he put down the receiver, the phone rang again. This time, he unplugged the cord.

He faced me. "Look, I've got a lot going on right now. How long are you in town?" His voice became smooth. "How about we discuss this over dinner?"

That's when Dante timed his entry.

The man saw his opportunity. Indicating Dante, he said, "I'm sorry, Allan, as you can see, I have a client." He tried to slip past me, out of his office.

"He's with me," I said.

The gallery owner appeared stunned. Dante gave him a stern wave.

"I don't plan on spending any time in Amsterdam," I said. "I've just come to pick up my paintings."

"I'm sorry; I don't have them."

I took out the fax I had sent him with a list of all the paintings and said, "Then you could pay for them. I've kept this on file since before the exhibition." I raised one eyebrow meaningfully. "It has all the prices."

I presented it with an authoritative snap, holding it out to him between my sticky doughnut fingers.

"Oh," he said. "I mean I don't have them here. They're all at my home."

I wasn't sure if this was a dodge, so I looked over at Dante.

Dante nodded as if to say *Let's go*, then spoke sternly, for the first time. "We don't want any trouble, just the paintings. Then we'll be on our way."

The gallery owner asked, "Do you have a car?"

"A truck."

"Then follow me."

I looked at Dante, who gave me an expression that said, *I'll take care of it.*

The gallery owner was between us but slipped through, rushing to his car. As he slammed the door, Dante and I ran to the truck to keep from losing him.

We followed for about 15 tense minutes, trying to keep his car in view, then stopped behind him at an apartment complex.

He showed us up the stairs and into a dark bedroom where we saw three crates. They were dusty and misshapen. I looked at the labeled boxes inside, tested them to make sure they weren't empty, and checked them all against my list.

As we left, the gallery owner muttered some excuse about an acrimonious divorce, but I was in no mood to hear about his personal problems.

I had just regained custody of my 20 orphans, which we carried out to the truck.

Doughnuts have never tasted so good.

With Dante's help, we had accomplished the improbable. It was an adventure, and I owed a lot to his initiative.

I was eager to start his painting. You can be sure a lot of gratitude went into that work.

EARTHQUAKE

One *early spring afternoon, a strange sensation gave* me goose bumps. Then came a sudden jolt, not the gradually escalating sway we had been accustomed to. It was fast moving and vertical. I stumbled my way to the doors and threw them open.

Windows chattered. Solid structures creaked and groaned. A bookend fell and crashed into the large glass jar of metallic leaf flakes I had used only moments before. It shattered in the impact, and the flakes flew up in a shimmering cloud of gold.

Next, the bookshelf that ran along the back wall fell forward onto where I had been working. I feared the studio would collapse, so I tried to move toward a more open area. The wall encircling the temple moved as if liquid, while the earth itself rolled like waves. It was difficult to stand, and as I bent my knees, I thought, This must be what it's like to surf.

The electrical lines crackled overhead, looped down, then snapped up as the telephone poles skewed and bowed. I looked back to see Saito-san clinging to our corner tree. During that nearly two minutes, the air was charged, liquids looked crazy, and the most solid things took on a liquid aspect. Heavy ceramic tiles rushed down the side of a roof, crashing row upon row onto the ground. Although some frames had broken, luckily, none of my artwork had been damaged.

Mami was supposed to be shopping at the outdoor market *Ameyoko* that originated as a black market area during wartime. It's crammed under the train tracks near Ueno station. I didn't want to imagine my wife there in the squeeze and jumble of people and produce. Dialing and redialing her cell phone was unsuccessful.

I ran to our house, our appointed meeting place. My son Ray was there. Fortunately, a tall bookcase that had fallen had missed him. The kitchen floor was a pile of broken crockery. Gen returned from school unfazed. Mami came back, and we all talked about the experience.

Finally, I was able to get through to Rick's school. They were holding the students in their safest room and would wait for me to pick him up.

I got on my bicycle and saw long lines of people waiting for blocks at bus stops, each line reaching beyond the beginning of the next line at the next stop. Passing by the electronics stores in Akihabara, I saw half-closed shutters and burly guards standing, arms folded, in front of piles of appliances that had been dashed from their shelves.

The bicycle ride took more than twice as long as the usual 40 minutes. The traffic lights were out, and obliging civilians were helping guide traffic. Rick was glad to see me and held me tight as he rode on the rack on the back of my bicycle. It was dark by the time we returned.

That night, we all slept in the studio.

The following month was difficult. Severed transportation lines made many foods unavailable. We slept in our clothes. The after-shocks were still strong and less than an hour apart.

The ad council aired public service announcements in the places where advertisements had normally been, because sponsors didn't want people to associate their products with the devastating images on the news. And there was nothing but news. Although the informa-tion was helpful, what we really wanted was entertainment. Weeks later, it was an emotional experience to see the first carton of milk appear on a store shelf.

For months after the earthquake, people from the neighborhood would stop by the studio, take a seat, and talk about their earthquake experience. It was the only thing on our minds, and the only way we could make sense of it was to talk and listen to the various stories.

My studio became the well side. This was not only therapeutic, but I could see how the many threads of the community wove together to become strong and resilient. People cleared broken tiles from the streets or replaced fallen gravestones without waiting to be asked.

At such times, people share food and chat "by the well." I am re-minded of Machida-san, who lives in a small wooden house halfway up the hill near my studio. At the end of each year, he makes a little figure of whatever animal represents the coming year and gives it to Seki-san at the top of the hill. This he does each year to thank her, because Seki-san's family shared their food with his family during the war.

As destructive as natural disasters are in Japan, the experience shows they are also a creative force. The strength of the bond in communities and depth of the national character have been forged and tempered by the hammering of earthquakes, floods, and fires.

Directly after airline flights resumed, foreigners who experienced the earthquakes went home in droves. Multinational corporations closed their Japanese branches, and for almost a year, only a small number of foreigners remained.

My Japanese friends asked if I would be going home too, but *this* was my home as it has been for more than 40 years. I have chosen to share the future with them, whatever it might be.

YAKUZA

Not long after the earthquake, our landlord sold the land under us and the tree over us.

We didn't learn until it was too late that they had sold it to the yakuza—the Japanese mafia. It was a stupid decision that affected seven households.

A letter arrived stating that from now on, we were to send our rent to a new account.

I thought we should gather to discuss the situation, so we met at my studio because it was large enough for us all.

It was almost like a party. Saito-san came an hour early to help me wipe down the table and set out the zabuton cushions Mr. Kobayashi had given me. She ran back and brought a basket full of wrapped cookies from her store to put on the table. Her eager anticipation was evident.

The daughter and son-in-law of Mr. Kobayashi came in from Urawa and renewed old acquaintances.

Abe-san entered, left her cane at the door, and greeted the other women by their childhood nicknames.

The young couple from the back of the triangle came, accompanied by the mother with whom they lived.

Horigome-san came in a light kimono.

My next-door neighbor whom we knew as *the Kid* wasn't interested.

Days before we met, the yakuza oozed their way into my studio. They arrived with thick pomade in their hair and wore tightly cinched black suits, dark sunglasses, and snakeskin shoes.

They sat in the middle of the room and squinted, looking at all corners of the room the way an appraiser would when assessing square footage. They were hyenas calculating the best angle from which to attack and devour their prey.

As my unsuspecting customers entered, the yakuza shamelessly unnerved them by simply lowering their sunglasses and glaring at their faces.

Some days they stayed outside carrying clipboards, pointing at the roof, or making sweeping gestures to indicate how the empty lot would look after tearing down my studio. The first time, I called the police after they left and asked what I should do. They gave me a number to call. I was to go to the back of my studio and quietly let the police know that *they* had returned.

Sometimes the police came too late. Or they might appear to be on their rounds and nonchalantly look in. The yakuza didn't dare be caught loitering, so that was usually enough to get them to leave.

The yakuza told Abe-san point-blank that they wanted her to move out by the end of the month. Her response was to shake her cane and ask, "Do you have children? Do you tell them that you throw grandmothers out of their homes? I don't know how you can sleep at night!" She pulled her cardigan tight and slammed the door on them.

We cheered at hearing of her plucky resistance.

They also told Horigome-san she could stay only another month.

Could they just kick us out like that? I had neighborhood friends ask if *I* was moving.

I did a little research and consulted with my father, who drew upon his legal and real estate experience. He was glad to help, and said that, though Japan was most likely different, many of the rights of tenants are universal, and I should start looking there. This was a great comfort to me as the stress of dealing with the yakuza mounted.

I found that as long as we paid our rent and continued to occupy and use the properties, they would have no legal right to throw us out. The deadlines they had set for us to leave were based only on the hope that we were ignorant of our rights.

A typical yakuza tactic was to make it so unpleasant to live there that we would leave of our own volition. They were not allowed to actively interfere with my business, but their mere presence was having an effect. They dug around behind my studio and severed my sewer line. They told me I was no longer allowed to maintain the property without their permission, so I had to close the studio and use the restroom of the neighboring cemetery while this was going on.

The yakuza wanted to combine our parcels of land and sell the whole section for a single large development at a greatly inflated price. We all decided to stick together and put up a united front of resistance. We were like a family, and together we would overcome this menace.

There were limits to my father's and my knowledge. We would need a Japanese lawyer familiar with these issues to defend us.

We met again the following week. Mrs. Kobayashi came in from Urawa and asked around until a neighbor introduced her to a lawyer, Mr. Mizuno.[42]

Saito-san called a meeting just to talk with him and then afterward we could tentatively think about whether or not we should ask him to help.

Mr. Mizuno arrived early. Once we were all there, he opened his misshapen briefcase, ran his fingers through the waves of his greasy hair and began with the words, "The reason I have invited you all here tonight ..."

He completely dominated the proceedings. Adjusting his glasses, Mr. Mizuno said that if any one of us gave up, it would make it more difficult for the rest of us to resist. "The yakuza will gradually chip away at you from the edges. If they can get one of you to leave, they'll tear your house down. A gaping hole between you and the others would make it more difficult to stay. Imagine the other side of your shared walls open to the elements."

It was an ugly thought, and he continued to frighten us with it.

"Don't worry," he said. "This kind of case is my specialty. This will be my crusade. I'll see what laws we can depend on to protect us."

Then Mr. Mizuno surprised us by saying the Kid wasn't going to come that night because he had been delinquent in paying his rent

---

42   This is not his real name.

for both properties for over three years.

That raised some eyebrows. The surprise was not about the Kid but rather this lawyer's disrespect for him. How could Mr. Mizuno divulge this private information?

He then turned to Saito-san, with another disclosure, "Your previous familial connections made it possible for you to go without paying rent in exchange for your work as superintendent. You can't expect that arrangement to continue with these characters. I love you people, and I will fight for you in the courts. Just keep up that united front!" He then explained how we were to pay him a monthly retainer fee.

He left. The dynamics of the previous meeting had shifted dramatically. We looked at each other, wondering if having a lawyer was really such a good idea.

The next week, Mr. Mizuno actually did call a meeting. He announced that, to his great disappointment and surprise, the Kid had cut a deal. On the condition that he leave immediately, the yakuza would find him an apartment nearby and forgive his unpaid rent.

The other families were moved by the emotions with which Mizuno made this announcement. He again made the appeal for us to stick together.

A few days later, the Kid moved to the far end of the block. Whenever he passed, I said hello, but he avoided my eyes. I learned that he had abandoned all his equipment in the tool shop and taken a job unloading boats of fish at the Tsukiji fish market.

Not long after that, the young family behind my studio learned they were going to have a baby. It made sense to take the money the yakuza offered them to leave. All moving expenses and fees were to be paid for. I asked if they were sure they wanted to do that.

"Yes. We're satisfied with the generous compensation because Mizuno sensei negotiated the deal."

I couldn't believe it. Mizuno had betrayed us.

I called a meeting for the next week. Mizuno appeared to be working against the interests of us, his clients. I wanted to discuss that, so I purposely did not invite him.

This time, Kobayashi-san voiced a concern. His place was empty and unused. The yakuza could argue that, without furniture there, he had already relinquished his right to tenancy. After retiring, he had taken up oil painting, so he could use the place as a weekend art studio. He would bring all his equipment and studio furniture and have an open house exhibition in the autumn. It sounded like a great idea, and I set him up with the local art-walk committee so that he could participate.

To my shock and surprise, an unknown woman, an architect, showed up at the next scheduled meeting. For some reason, she had a thorough knowledge of the situation and was prepared with a proposal. The question that bothered me was how she knew so much. Her proposal required tearing down all the houses and building a four-story structure that we could all share. There would be more space, an expanded studio for me, and a medical staff for the older women.

She proudly spread out her plans in front of us. They were impressive, but they meant tearing down the homes in which these people had been born and raised.

I also noticed, with alarm, that it meant our beloved cedar tree would be cut down. It would no longer fit with their scheme.

I told everyone it was late. Though there were other matters, we would have to save them for another time. I watched the architect leave, and as the rest were looking for their shoes, I asked them who had invited the architect.

"How did she know our names and about all of our various needs? Who invited her?"

In a chorus, they all said, "We thought *you* did!"

It was just as I feared. Apparently, the architect was acting as the eyes and ears of Mizuno. So much time had passed since the previous meeting that he must have wondered why he wasn't invited. The architect had gone to Kobayashi-san and cleverly told her she forgot what time the meeting was. Kobayashi-san gave her the information, assuming I had invited her.

When my father called me for an update, I told him about the architect. We referred to her and her assistant as the *harpies*. It was cathartic to discuss this with someone who could provide advice and encouragement.

One morning, I saw the architect quietly slip out of the door of the Kid's workshop. What was she doing in there? Behind her was a man with long gray hair, a puffy face, and protruding eyes. He gave me a business card from the pocket of his khaki jacket. He was her mentor—an architect specializing in preservation.

He told me he was going to take out the wall over there. I would have to move the toilet in my studio to the front to accommodate the changes he was going to make to the shared sewer system. The frontage of my studio would have to be moved back to accommodate the construction vehicles that they would need. The street was so narrow the fire trucks wouldn't be able to pass, so they'd need to report to the local government that my studio was a fire hazard.

I had had enough. I asked if they realized they were trespassing. Had they gotten permission from the owners? I could hardly believe their answer:

"From the yakuza, you mean? Yes, we did."

Who negotiates with yakuza? What were they thinking! Would they try these same tactics to make me leave?

They were not going to impose their grand ideas on me! Stunned, I had to do something. I pointed to the cracked beam overhead, telling them it was dangerous, and they'd better go. The thought of having this pushy harpy and her condescending mentor next door, constantly goading me, made my stomach churn.

Early one morning, angry shouting behind my studio shattered the harmony of the neighborhood. I threw on my clogs and followed the wild sounds to Horigome-san's place. Yakuza stood at her front door, barking insanely threatening sounds.

Verbal threats are against the law, so they had adopted an even more frightening animalistic growl—all the more terrifying for its irrational eeriness. The yakuza were not permitted to open a door or hold it open, but they couldn't be prevented from ringing the doorbell or knocking. Horigome-san supported herself by grasping the doorjamb. Her face was pale, and I sensed her rapid breathing under her kimono.

I could think of only one way to extricate this 90-year-old woman. It was to say, "Oh! Horigome-san, if you don't go now, you'll be late for your doctor's appointment." I then took her around to my studio and sat her down in a quiet back room. She needed some water and a moment to recover.

After that, we moved the doorbell ringer to the back of her house so I could hear it and check who it was before she opened the door. This seemed to work. The yakuza were not going to waste their efforts on her if I appeared each time.

I needed to prevent the harpies from purchasing the shop next door, and I needed to do it fast. If they learned I was the one who wanted it, they would recognize my motivation and charge a high price for it. The yakuza were also known for making phony contracts to dupe people out of their money.

I found a real estate agent to purchase the land with the shop on it. He did so on my behalf while keeping my name a secret.

I had a simple plan to detect trespassers. Just inside the door, I closed the shop curtains and arranged them with precision.

A few days later, I saw the curtains had been disturbed. The architect was there. She was inside with her harpies. She had a clipboard with graph paper on it and was sketching out a floorplan and measurements.

I asked if she had gotten permission from the owners.

"The yakuza? Oh, yes. I talked to them and got permission," she replied.

I had caught her in a lie. I was the owner now, and I could lie as well.

I said, "This place has been condemned. The local government says, for safety reasons, no one can enter. Shall I call someone to find out whether you should be here?"

She left quickly. I had a good laugh about it that night with my father.

I thought I had gotten rid of the lawyer Mizuno, but I was mistaken.

He had allowed no one to see his interactions with the yakuza. All the time, he had been playing both sides. He was acting on behalf of the yakuza and pretending to work tirelessly for our benefit. His careful strategy ensured him of whatever percentage of the take he could finagle by keeping all sides in the dark.

With the harpy, he devised a nasty but brilliant plot: They discovered that two-thirds of the spreading cedar tree had grown into the public land of the road. The local government had never considered it an issue, but Mizuno and the harpies created a problem where none existed. They pretended that the local government had threatened to cut down the tree for encroaching onto the public road. They formulated a wave of publicity with a phony campaign they ironically called *Save Our Tree.* In actuality, the campaign was designed to threaten our beautiful tree's existence and to get us all to move. Nevertheless, with such a name, unknowing fans of our tree gathered signatures and money that ended up paying Mizuno and the harpies for their efforts.

We experienced an overwhelming outpouring of support, but had no way of expressing how unhelpful it actually was. The attention brought real estate speculators, like buzzards circling over fresh carrion.

A series of drawings I had made of the tree over a 20-year period proved to me the tree was thriving—growing at a surprising rate.

Did the tree belong to the city because two-thirds of the trunk had expanded into public lands? Did the tree belong to Saito-san because her grandmother had it in a little pot on her land? And did the potted plant belong to successive generations? Did the tree belong to the yakuza, who owned the land wherein the core of the tree and the original pot had been placed?

One spring, Saito-san's store was open later than usual, and I peeked in. An officious-looking woman filled the space normally reserved for customers. At the sight of Saito-san's rigid expression, I had the worst of premonitions. I shot her a look of panic.

I later learned she had signed away her ownership and responsibility for the tree to the phony Save Our Tree organization headed by the harpy architect.

This betrayal was accomplished by order of the court on the recommendation of Mizuno—our own attorney.

It felt like a stake in my heart. Now that the yakuza officially owned the glorious cedar tree on our corner, there was nothing they couldn't do. They could have leverage over us by threatening its existence.

A few months into this oppressive situation, the local government created a new designation for the protection of streetscapes of cultural importance. Our tree was the first to be designated. Protection by the local government would ensure its continued good health.

The winner in this contest of wills was none other than the great Himalayan cedar itself—the protector of our corner.

No More Time-Traveling
Clients from Mars

Dad's logic helped me immensely during the plague of the yakuza. He was able to guide me through some universal legal concepts that would apply to Japan as well. He had excellent practical advice on how to resist and cope. It was the flowering of a new period of our relationship. I needed him, and the conversations were not traumatic. Instead, they relieved stress.

Around that time, I asked for his help making sense of some strange contracts for a new commission. A multinational organization[43] ordered a series of murals for a facility in Japan, and I needed to sign a contract with the headquarters in the United States. Though I was less familiar with contracts in English, this one seemed bizarre.

---

43   One of the stipulations of the contract was that I not mention the organization by name.

I sent it to Dad, and we went through it line by line.

He confirmed it was legendary. I was to sign away the copyright to the artwork and its image throughout the whole universe and for all eternity.

Usually, at the very least, the artist was able to retain the right to use photographs of the work for promotional purposes. Not even that was allowed.

We had a lot of fun laughing about the implications of the contract I was to sign. Did they fear I might sell bootleg replicas of the work to time travelers on Mars?

The paintings were to go in the corporation's new private building in a large city in Japan. I was shown the blueprints. The paintings were to be so large that I couldn't spread them out in my studio. I had to paint them in sections and hoped they would match.

Over a decade before, the organization had commissioned a painting of a maple tree for another facility, and they had been pleased with that painting.

The interior designers were pleasant to work with and, to help me make my proposals, sent me samples of the carpeting, wallpaper, wood, and even the upholstery.

I proposed a set of two old, venerable pine trees. One was to be painted with an angular shape for the branches and the other with a more curved shape.

They were to be painted only in white with a warm silvery gold leaf background. The metallic leaf would give depth, causing the painted portions to appear to float in space. The paintings were to decorate the walls above the entrance so one would need to look up to see them.

I proposed to use an amalgamation of gold and platinum. But unfortunately, I had made the mistake of appearing in person at the gold leaf shop. The craftspeople who made it decided not to sell to me. They said it was made according to a proprietary secret, so they would only sell to professional nihonga masters.

We learned the hard way that my wife should have gone there in my place. We have since printed up a business card attesting to her being a representative of the *Edokoro* Art Sanctuary. When they don't have to see my foreign face, it's easier for them to treat my studio as a proper nihonga establishment.

I told the clients there was a substitution I could make that would be a similar color. I was to go ahead, using this other kind of metallic leaf.

After preparing the panels, and the months it took to lay on the gold leaf, I started painting. Then the architects called and told me an unforeseen air duct would have to go through the bottom six inches of the mural.

I had to start over.

62

SAVED FROM THE DUMPSTER

My parents needed me to help clear out their storage unit. They were storing a great quantity of my art that had accumulated from museum exhibitions in the States. The funds for returning all of the works to Japan had run out. There were also over a dozen six-foot-by-six-foot paintings from my Carnegie Mellon years and earlier.

I arranged this trip to coincide with the opening of an exhibition there. I dreaded the trip, knowing I would have to choose between tossing artwork or finding some way to ship them to Japan before the week was up. I went to stay with my parents and was prepared to photograph each work that might need to go to the dumpster. In addition to that, I was also not looking forward to the subtly disapproving suggestions surrounding my beard and clothing.

On the day of the opening party of the exhibition, I was getting ready when I received some criticism for how I looked: "Washington,

DC, is a conservative place. Don't you think this Japanese outfit is a bit much?"

My father heard that and defended me. He said that it was my big day, and I should be able to wear whatever I wanted.

I couldn't believe my ears. I thanked him for this. With it, the two of us entered new and unfamiliar territory.

The next day at the storage unit, all my father's reactions were completely unexpected. "Oh, you don't want to throw that one away, do you?

"I really like that one.

"I had forgotten about that.

"I bet we could find a place to hang that somewhere."

What a surprise! Why was he telling me these things now? I loved hearing them, and we were getting along so well. Whether or not my father understood this jumble of artwork, I felt strongly, and for the first time, that he genuinely *appreciated* them. I felt a corner had turned in our relationship. I relished the thought of future heart-to-heart talks like we'd had when I was much younger.

A few months after I returned to Tokyo, we had one of those talks. It was my birthday. A three-hour telephone conversation. It was glorious. He said if he were younger and had a grasp of the language, he'd want to live in Japan too. And what a wonderful life I had made for myself there. He loved thinking of me painting in my studio. What would I paint next? And how was that commission coming along?

He spoke approvingly of my wife and boys, one by one, and how good a husband and father I had been.

It was a silly, fun, validating, confirming, energizing conversation—and one of my best memories ever.

63

THE CALL

The next day, I was still on a high from our conversation. The phone rang. Was it Dad? How odd. He was never up this late. No, it was Mom on the other end. Her voice was controlled.

"Your father has had a stroke. He's been hospitalized, and I called you as soon as possible. Can you tell Page and Adam? We won't really know anything until we get the results of the tests. I'll tell you the minute I know."

I hung up the phone and immediately called my brother and sister.

I flew to the States as soon as I could. I had been told he had mo-tor-skill issues that made it hard for him to move. They also affected his eating and speech. I knew they had opened his skull to operate on his brain to relieve the pressure. I steeled myself at his hospital door.

Seeing myself in a hall mirror, I realized I hadn't trimmed my beard in three months. I hadn't considered what my father's reaction to it might be until that moment.

Dad was awake. He saw me and recognized me immediately. Happily beckoning me in, he pointed to my chin, giving me an approving smile and a thumbs-up.

I had brought some books with me to read to him. They were books he had entertained us with at the beach when we were children. I left Sherlock Holmes in the bag, for fear it might give him bad dreams.

In years past, we had laughed together over the writings of P. G. Wodehouse, which turned out to be just right. No problem was so great it couldn't be solved with the application of a bit of Jeeves's incomparable gray matter. I would stop if he tired. But every time I checked, he kept giving me the thumbs-up for more.

In time, Dad was transferred to rehabilitation; there was hope.

My commission's deadline could not be ignored. When the week was up, I gave him a kiss, told him I loved him, and said goodbye. Mom was with him in the hospital every day. They allowed her to set up a Christmas tree there. I pled with God to help my father recover or at least let him live. Could I deal with this?

In the spring, Dad's condition suddenly worsened. I tried to get a flight, but nothing was available for a week. Adam put his phone to Dad's ear, and I was able to say goodbye to him one more time. Mom is my example, but Dad was my motivation.

I was numb. At the airport, when immigration asked the purpose of my trip, a sob caught in my throat. I was going to my father's funeral.

I didn't really have the time to take off work, but nothing could keep me away.

I went to the funeral and said *hello* and *thank you* to all the nice people—many of whom I loved dearly and hadn't seen in decades. Someone introduced himself and said that he had heard good things about the paintings I was working on. How did he know? I shook his hand but with no awareness of what I was saying.

All the while, I wanted only to sit in the moment with thoughts of my father. I couldn't feel anything. In the casket, I saw what looked like a sculpture of Dad.

At the cemetery, after friends and family receded, Mom seemed bewildered but spoke for us all. Choking, she said, "I don't want to leave him here."

I needed time, but I had no time. I had to return and finish the commission in my Tokyo studio. Sitting on the bridge over the expanse of cream-colored metal, I painted. The simplicity of using only white paint meant that I needed to be careful of the tonalities and keep the brushwork fresh.

The pine tree gradually became my tribute to my father and a portrait of him. The other pine tree painting became one of my mother. As I worked around the reflective creamy-silver-and-white paint, tears fell on the surface.

I ate and napped and wept on that bridge for months. My life was there on that bridge as I put down my feelings and memories of my dad.

That white pine had become my conduit to the heaven I was sure my father now occupied.

At the base of the tree, I painted a grouping of small seedlings. These were my wife and children, my siblings, and me. We had been shaded and protected by our father, this great tree. I wanted to feel that we could at least be there in the painting, under his protection.

Before I was even finished with that project, the corporation commissioned me to do additional paintings for the lobby. Would I send in a proposal?

A few years earlier, I had done some sketches of a project that ended up being cancelled. I emailed photographs of them, unable to spend much time with this new distraction.

They were approved.

Could they be ready in two months? I said that would be a really tight schedule, but I thought I could make it.

Not yet finished with the other two paintings, I now had to start the new pair for the lobby. These were to be in a complicated combination of colors. At six-feet-by-eight-feet, they were much smaller than the murals, but even though they were smaller, they would hang much closer to the viewer and therefore require more detail.

I needed to turbocharge my efficiency in painting. Mami brought me daily changes of clothes and delivered spinach curry and samosas. Otherwise, I would not have known night from day. I slept when I couldn't work anymore and worked the rest of the time.

I told myself it took a lot of heat and a lot of pressure to make a diamond. I needed to accept these extreme conditions.

One day, I received a call. The lobby paintings would have to be sent to headquarters for approval before they could be accepted.

I painted right up until the minute my shipper, Sakai-san, came with his truck to collect, pack, and send them. He and Mami fanned it dry as I painted one last place. Without even the time to breathe a sigh of relief, I resumed work on the pine tree murals.

With the lobby paintings crossing the Pacific to get approved, I worked on finishing the pine tree murals. I would have to arrange their delivery and hanging. Because they were to be hung up above the entry doors, it was going to take a feat of engineering to manage.

I called in a man who built and installed signs and billboards strong enough to withstand hurricanes and earthquakes. His side business was installing large, usually public, works of art.

I hadn't seen the sun in days.

It took a day of travel to show him the site and the facilities. While we were there, the workmen were hanging an immense chandelier with use of a scaffolding system. He asked if the scaffolding would be available when we were expected to hang the paintings. It would not. In order to use the scaffolding, we would have to hasten the day of installation. Those three days were going to hurt.

At that news, my fingers went numb. I took the last train back to Tokyo. I was grateful for the conductor who woke me at the last stop, Tokyo station.

With three days eliminated, I desperately needed to create a strategy to finish on time.

The day before I was to deliver the paintings, a truck arrived with a huge delivery from corporate headquarters.

I didn't understand. Why had the lobby paintings been delivered to *me*, not to the site? It meant I would have to arrange the last leg of this delivery as well.

The package seemed unnecessarily large.

Fortunately, I peeked inside. For some strange reason, the paintings were framed in heavy, foot-wide wooden frames. They might have been fine for a Western-style painting, but this frame swallowed up their delicacy.

I had planned to frame them with three-quarter-inch wood to match the lobby's wood paneling. It was to be the kind of frame one would expect on a folding-screen painting with gold fittings on the corners.

I didn't have the time to remove the unwieldy frame. I would have to do it at the site. It took the last spurt of effort just to finish the paintings in time.

The next day, my delivery man, Sakai-san, came. He loaded the truck with the two pine murals that I had dismantled and the unanticipated payload of the lobby paintings. I packed up the framing equipment and some white paint, just in case.

I slept on the plane, and when I arrived, the installer was at the site and had already climbed the scaffolding. We would need nine people to raise the painting.

Once I put the mural panels together, I could see places where parts of the painting didn't connect properly.

While the workmen were at lunch, I warmed my deer protein in a sink of hot water. For a container, I found a beverage can and cut off the top. In it, I mixed the protein and pigment to make the paint to fix the connections.

The walls were measured. Then, in the process of putting the cleats on the walls and on the backs of the paintings, someone brushed one of the cleats against the surface and made an indented line near where I had painted the seedlings. I had to add another seedling there, to the bottom of the tree—an additional sibling.

Once that was finished, we put on our gloves and moved the painting into position. With an orchestrated heave, we lifted the mural, cautiously holding it in place while we inched it up the side of the scaffolding.

When the crew was at dinner, I ran out to the garage where the lobby paintings were, took off the clunky frames, put on the new wood with the gold fittings, and handed them off to be hung. The project took everything I had emotionally and physically.

When I finished the project, I collapsed. I hardly remember the rest of the year. I spent most of it sleeping and vomiting. My hands shook.

I had poured the essence of my father into these paintings. Now that they were gone, the loneliness and loss were more acute. Until now, I had had no choice but to defer mourning the loss of my father.

I isolated myself in a small area above the studio and lost almost 70 pounds. I was so weak I could barely stand and had to rest after walking across the room.

My studio was "closed for repairs until further notice." I had difficulty swallowing, and other bodily functions threatened to fail in alarming ways.

Every morning, my wife pulled back the heavy curtains quietly, so as not to wake me. When food from the day before went uneaten, she checked to make sure I was still breathing.

I couldn't see myself living through this, and I didn't care.

One night in my sweat-soaked sheets, I had a dream of sitting on a couch with Dad. We were talking and laughing happily. It wasn't a real conversation. It was an impression. I heard his voice clearly, and his affirmation shook my frame.

Yes, he said.

That was all, but it changed everything for me.

I had to take control of my health. Previously, I had been asked to paint a fan for a Theatre Nohgaku[44] production by Elizabeth Dowd. Would it be ready on time?

I had previously painted backdrops for my Noh drama friends, and I couldn't say no. I couldn't hold myself upright and had to lean over a portable armrest to focus my strength and determination on my hand. The nerves in my hand would misfire, causing me to jerk wildly or drop the brush.

It took immense amounts of concentration. Taking breaks and watching as broad areas of color were filling in, I soon remembered what it was like to paint. My hand still shook, and I needed both hands for a time.

When I could sit on the bench outside, the sunlight felt good again. Combining colors felt new. I experimented with how the angle of light would play on the colors. I could see my recovery in the progress of the fan. By the time I finished, I enjoyed the challenge of painting again and could hardly wait to start my next project. Painting once again defined my sense of well-being and purpose. I remembered the interview I heard in my youth: "I would die if I couldn't paint." But in my case, I'm alive because I *can* paint!

A pianist friend said my father sounded much like the typical Japanese company man. "My experience is similar," he said. "He probably brought his corporate leadership skills home with him. In Japan, a father who softens loses respect and ceases to be a father." Hearing this was cathartic. I finally understood.

---

44   Theatre Nohgaku is the first professional Noh drama troupe to be traditionally trained in Noh and also write and present performances in English.

I am forever grateful for the motivation my father was for me. It is a lifelong gift, and I draw on it every day.

I remember our relationship being fraught with emotion. There were many lost opportunities. I know now that he must have seen me as a complexity of confusion; I didn't appear to operate within the constraints of logic.

In hindsight, the scarcity of his approval was a motivation. It was in fact huge. There were times I was horrified to catch myself muttering, "I'll show you!" under my breath as I painted.

I have had plenty of company. I remember an interview with an Olympic athlete who was asked about his motivation. He appreciated his Soviet rival; without him he would not have aimed so high, and his efforts would have ended earlier.

I may not have been the best artist in Mr. Bartman's high school art class, but I was the most determined. I remember being stressed and hearing Dad say, "There is always someone out there trying harder." I understood. Not only would I have to try harder than anyone else, but I would also have to do it smarter. Only now as I write, I realize he was trying, in his way, to get me to compete with myself.

I keep the hiking boots he used when he was in the forest service inside the door of my studio. It looks as if he has just removed them and is looking around inside.

THE PURVEYOR'S HOBBY

One day, Mrs. Matsushita was measuring out the *Enji* maroon pigment I requested. That luscious color always made my mouth water.

"Well, that's that," she said. "You've just purchased the last there is."

"You mean for now, right?" I laughed nervously.

"Sorry, I don't have enough to fill your order."

"You'll be getting more, of course. I mean ... won't you?"

"No. The family that made it died out without an apprentice."

This incredible pigment had been protected for generations. In Arita, I had seen the graves of craftsmen who perished protecting their secrets. No one else could reproduce this unusual color. The secret behind creating this pigment had died with them.

After a few years of my patronage, Mr. Matsushita one day invited me to see something interesting on the third floor. Was that an excuse to get away from contending with his wife?

Though he was a retailer, he dabbled in creating pigments from lapis lazuli at a good price. A huge steel platform and a heavy stainless-steel cylinder took me by surprise. He rolled the gigantic cylinder back and forth across chunks of lapis lazuli, crushing them with each pass.

The vibrations shook the building, and I realized this was the origin of the thunderous sound I had thought was the subway.

He showed me how veins of calcium seeped into the seams of lapis. To create a vivid royal blue, he had to remove the calcium with acid. Passing the stone crumbs through a series of seven sieves, the finest powder was eventually separated.

I felt privileged that he would show me this secret process and let me live! As the grains comprising the pigment became smaller, the pulverized rocks appeared lighter. With a microscope, he showed me that the fine grains of powder were just as dark as the large original rock. I could see the sparkle of the tiniest facets. The actual color of the rock was not lighter at all. But because of the light glinting off these miniaturized gems, it only appeared so. Thus, even finely ground black obsidian can be used to make white paint.

Matsushita-san had witnessed the Depression and then the privations after the war. Because of that, he did his best to support artists by purchasing leftover scraps of lapis and malachite from *Okachimachi*, the nearby jewelry district. From these he processed the most expensive but essential colors for his cash-strapped patrons.

One day in Okachimachi, I saw lapis lazuli scraps for sale by weight. I was surprised and touched to realize Matsushita-san had been selling the pigments he made at cost. I then remembered his enigmatic smile when he said that making this pigment was just a hobby.

I had uncovered his secret kindness.

The familiar bickering of Matsushita-san and his wife continued. Even so, I found Purveyors of Joy to be an appropriate name for the shop.

At this writing, it has been about 10 years since his death. The shop is sadly quiet when I go there now.

With pleasure, I imagine Mr. Matsushita shouting gruffly to his wife from above, "Woman, where are you? I'm waiting!"

RED AND WHITE

The longer I am in Japan, the more my concept of time changes. In Tokyo, the facade of my present studio was built in the 1730s. In the district where my studio is, the average temple is around three hundred years old.

I buy my paper from Yokoo-san at Masumi. When he says it will last for a thousand years, he knows.

The paper workshop he deals with has been in the same family for over thirteen hundred years. They have retained samples of those papers and know exactly which materials and techniques must be used to make paper that will withstand time.

One beautiful pigment comes from my friend Tsuji-san. He lives in a low timbered house in Imari, the ancient capital of Japanese porcelain. He prepares the glazes for workshops that dot the community. His specialty is a fine bright-red iron oxide pigment.

He makes it by putting iron filings into almost a hundred ceramic jars of about a gallon each. Every day he gently pours the water out, careful not to disturb the iron, and replaces it with new water that oxidizes the filings.

The jars are circled under the veranda of his small dooryard garden. He calls them *his children.* The oldest ones have been tended and cared for every day for the last 90 years. Every year he sells a jar's worth of the pigment, and every year he begins the process again with new filings.

Tsuji-san is about the 24th generation to do this. He has not met the ancestor who first watered the filings he is now selling, and he will not know the posterity who will sell his pigment. But he is glad to pass the baton in this multigenerational marathon.

Another beautiful paint is the white made from oyster shells. It would be easy to grind the shells for pigment. But the shells are made of thin layers of nacre. Grinding them would cause the pearlescent layers to eventually come apart, causing the paint to flake off. The solution is to let nature take care of the process herself.

Oyster shells are laid outside to receive the sun, rain, and snow for 80 years. This causes all the layers to flake off gently, as a white powder. The powder is so fine that, to be used as paint, it must be treated differently than most other pigments. We add deer protein little by little to the powder, kneading until it feels like clay. It must be slammed against a plate a hundred times to ensure the adhesive protein has coated every granule evenly.

GONE WITH THE WIND

When we were away from Tokyo, we heard worrisome news about a typhoon that was due to strike. Having had no warning before our departure, we didn't prepare the studio.

At the same time, I did receive some good news. The Smithsonian wrote to inform me they had finally scheduled my exhibition. Because the museum had been used for a government-related reception, years of scheduling needed to be rearranged. At last, it was all coming together.

I had just completed my one last project, a folding-screen painting in gold. If the museum didn't receive it within the next few months, it would be too late. But I would have no trouble getting it there in time. The posters of it were already being printed.

Upon returning to my Tokyo studio, I was stunned. In my absence, the typhoon had broken open a window, and the painting for the

Smithsonian had been damaged. Scrubbed by the wind and driving rain, much of the right half was scarred, and the gold leaf was loosened and folded down upon itself.

It was no longer acceptable.

Creating a replacement would be an opportunity to revisit the original theme of the painting, and I hoped to improve upon it. On the other hand, each painting required approval. I could only hope the museum would accept a painting they had not originally planned on exhibiting.

When I called, the museum asked why I couldn't take a photograph and send it to them. Inasmuch as the painting didn't exist yet, I could truthfully say it was temporarily unavailable.

Unable to see the photograph, they wanted to know what it was like. I explained it was from the same series, using essentially the same materials.

Maybe I could paint a new one and get it approved in time for new posters to be printed.

But it would be dicey.

67

TYPHOON

Japan is no longer able to ignore climate change. One autumn, the typhoons were record-breaking in number as well as in strength. A particularly strong one shook the studio, and the next day I found out Saito-san had spent an exhausting night pushing back against her doors, which had threatened to come off their rails.

The next week, news commentators predicted another typhoon with even higher wind velocity. We knew this one would be far worse when they spoke in terms of hectopascals. Mami and I taped the windows. Warning messages aimed at specific localities were transmitted by the local government. Anyone living below such and such an embankment should evacuate.

That dark afternoon, Saito-san and I screwed plywood to windows and doors. I greased the rails and pulled the steel garage doors down across the front of my studio. Motorcycles were tied down and cars were moved off the street. Police with bullhorns reprimanded people for leaving their homes to buy supplies. There was a curfew, and no one was allowed outside.

We hunkered down as well as we could. The din of my steel casements chattering in the violent wind woke me. At about 2 a.m., I heard through the wall what sounded like a plywood board flying loose and hitting concrete with a crack.

The groan of the wind kept me awake as the percussion of gravel or hard rain slapped against the studio shutters. It pressed against them until they bowed inward.

Soon sleep overtook exhaustion. Was this the end, or was it the eye of the storm and therefore only the first half of the ordeal? I took the opportunity to sleep, then woke to the sound of urgent voices outside. Crawling out from under the shutter, I saw a clutch of people talking in the light.

Of the five trunks of our Himalayan cedar, one of them had cracked just above the roofline of Saito-san's store and had fallen exactly into the road in front of it. Laid out, the tips of the branches brushed up against my studio. They completely blocked the doors, obscuring the front of Saito-san's store and Abe-san's house. Coming out their back doors, they picked their way toward the heavy green boughs and saw how they filled the street.

The thick branches were littered with garbage cans, a bicycle, and broken glass. The trunk and the thick skirting of its boughs had protected our houses from the flying debris scattered over it. It was like a mother driving with her arm extended in front of her child in anticipation of a collision. People remarked on its valorous act of protection on our behalf.

Our tree made the news. It represented the brutality of the typhoon that so many people in Tokyo had experienced. Police line tape was stretched from my studio's columns. There was no telling whether any other newly weakened branches might also come down during the night.

Local government representatives told Abe-san and Saito-san that, until the trunk and branches were cleared away, they would have to be evacuated to the local elementary school. The government had already prepared cots and bedding.

They both objected strenuously. They were not going to spend the night away from home. Saito-san said, if the tree was going to hurt her, she was okay with that.

I offered to have them spend the night in my studio. They recounted the experience of the typhoon. They also spoke of an activist who had prevented the construction of ugly concrete embankments the year before. The inadequate earthen berms had been on the news because they had collapsed that night and caused flooding. That activist was now the target of recriminations.

Officials brought rigid vacuum-packed bedding for my "evacuees." Saito-san sneaked back into her store to bring back some rice crackers, and when no one was looking, Abe-san got some tea and a cushion to sit on.

People stopped by to check up on us and to lament the damage to the tree. It seemed strange having the huge branches, once so high in the air, down on our level. It took the local government four days of intense work to clear the road.

Gradually, life returned to a sort of normal.

One-fifth of the spreading canopy was gone, and I couldn't accustom myself to the sun's glare over the now-naked part of our street. I sat on the bench in front of my studio every day, looking at the tree as I always had and sent it my thoughts: You can weather this coming winter, then send out your new shoots of green. Let your branches extend into the open spaces. We will get over this trauma.

Every day I looked up to tell the tree it could heal, but as days passed, the murky drops of sap on the street under the wound grew in number. Where one of the five trunks had once been, sap was still painfully weeping from the site of the dismemberment.

People asked what was going to happen to the tree.

It would grow back. It would go on. What else would there be? People kept speculating.

One day, as I sat on my bench, I overheard half a conversation. "If it could happen once, it could happen again." And I wondered how the force of a typhoon might treat our cedar now. I was not going to think about it. The thought was just too awful.

Each day I sat under the tree to sketch or read the news.

Social upheaval and political unrest increased. Faith in institutions was weakened. A pandemic filled the news, then filled our cities. What could we hold on to?

I looked up at the tree.

I know you can push out new branches in the spring. We've got to gather our strength if we are to thrive. You can do it.

Approximately a year after the event, the local authorities chose a tree doctor to look at our Himalayan cedar. We hoped to hear the tree would recover. Surely, they would do nothing more than trim it so the wind could pass through safely.

This would make sense. It could maintain its general shape. Perhaps they would thin the places where the growth was at its thickest. That would preserve the structural integrity of the tree while still maintaining its balance. I tried to resign myself to the thought. I knew it was for the best, though it would be painful to watch. I understood a tree doctor had been carefully chosen by the local government.

One morning I was awakened by chainsaws. They had begun the process of choosing which branches to fell. Each one was attached to a pulley and lowered carefully.

My heart pounded, and I felt strangely ill. I couldn't watch one more day of this. If I were to say something or recommend preserving as many branches as possible, I might be blamed for any future damage that might occur. Early the next morning I left, to maintain my health.

A week later, I received some photographs, but I couldn't bring myself to look at them. Now only two of the five thick trunks remain, and very few branches of those are left. Open and stark, a human-made misery has robbed our quiet world of all shade. Gone is the subtlety of modulated color. There is no symbiosis of humankind and tree; only the evidence of a brutal truncation.

I don't know if the tree will survive or if I can love her the same way again. Not even one-twentieth of the green remains, but this greatest heartbreak is not her fault. I don't want her to see me avert my eyes from the evil disfigurement.

Ironically, the local government, which declared the tree an important cultural asset, paid for half of this. The other half came from the Save Our Tree fund.

I felt betrayed.

I have had time to think. To many, this is a minor thing when compared to the scale of human suffering in the world. Nevertheless, something beautiful has been lost—something that provided joy and solace.

The lush green growth of this great tree had brought me to Yanaka. It feels as though there is too much change for our corner to endure. In just a few days, the gentle nurture of a century has been destroyed.

After the death of my father and having to rebuild my health, I feel much closer to this tree somehow. Our futures feel entwined. I will accept how things are now and do what I can. If I maintain my health, perhaps I, too, can be someone's solace.

Now I must be a tree and provide shade.

Thanks to the many portraits I have painted of this magnificent tree, I can show visitors to our neighborhood how it once looked—and what it will always mean to us.

It will remain forever fixed in my memory.

68

THANK YOU FOR YOUR SHADE

Okage *literally means "honored shade." The image is* of a great tree protecting a young seedling from the hot sun or pelting rain. It is with this shade that the seedling is able to mature. The word suggests a responsibility for both the watcher and the person being watched.

It has a significant part in Japanese life. This vertical relationship suggests a proud connection. The caring associated with the young person of promise and being thought worthy of such care are equal distinctions.

As I took my son Ray to his first day of preschool, he showed me how he intuitively understood this. He said, "Just a minute, Daddy. I need to stop here." He walked into the pigment store.

Like a little adult, he said to Sugita-san, "Thank you for your careful watch over me and my family. Today will be my first day of school. I hope to live up to your expectations."

I was aware of the expectations my professor had for me. As a student chosen by Professor Kayama, it was a privilege to study under his careful watch. It is an ongoing responsibility to carry on his name, give credit, represent him well, and bring honor to his wisdom as a teacher.

I understood that his accepting me carries with it his recommendation. He wanted to be sure I learned the best of his wisdom; I needed to return his trust by earnest practice and study.

One day he called me into his office. It was humbling, and I feared for what the reason might be.

He motioned for me to sit down. "I thought you should know of my desires for you. I've seen your potential and think you could bring needed stimulation to the art of nihonga."

Hearing this directly from someone so important to the nihonga world took me by surprise. I had entered the office somewhat cowed and left it feeling a few inches taller.

When I had an exhibition at the International Forum, an online financial magazine, *Nikkei BP*, ran an article on it. The reporter had asked my professor to make a comment on my work.

He said he thought no one else could use metallic leaf to this level. This happened just a few months before his death.

It was the last I was to hear from Kayama sensei in this life, and his words left me with a sense of responsibility. When he left this world, he was in his mid-70s, and it caught many of us off guard. He would no longer show up unexpectedly at my exhibitions. I was no longer able to ask for advice, or feedback. I could no longer report to him the birth of a new son or exchange exhibition announcements and New Year's greetings.

It was odd how concretely I felt the absence of something over-head. I no longer had an example to follow or a champion, should I be criticized. I had lost someone to look up to. I felt exposed and alone.

After Professor Kayama's death, I was asked to stand at the en-trance to receive condolatory offerings from the funeral attendees. While doing so, I thought of what a great privilege it had been to grow under his influence—and to say one last time to Professor Kayama, "Thank you for your shade."

I try to honor his name through my work.

Now it is my turn to be the tree providing shade, as others have so generously done for me.

COLLABORATION

Many people I have collaborated with also know and have worked with one another. A beautiful network of friendship develops as we share a common aim and overcome difficulties along the way.

I was once invited to a vocal concert to meet the piano accompanist about a possible album cover. While visiting with him afterward, I met the jazz vocalist Susan Osborn, who had sung for the opening of the Winter Olympics in Nagano. We immediately became friends.

At a tea salon in Sendai, I met the *butoh* dancer Oyama Tokiko, the early benefactor of Yayoi Kusama. We collaborated on many performances after that. I had been asked to present one of my folding-screen paintings at the American embassy; the painting was also to be used as a backdrop for a concert to be held that same day.

There at the embassy, I found Bruce Heubner, a friend I had originally met at the university. He had been performing on the *shakuha-chi*, a type of Japanese bamboo flute. It turned out he had performed with Oyama Tokiko *and* Susan Osborn.

Oyama-san had an idea. Instead of displaying my art as the backdrop for various performances, the collaboration could go a step further. She had a brilliant idea and found just the right venue in Sendai. It was an arena-like stage, with box seating arranged in a cylindrical shape—more vertical than horizontal. The audience would look down on us.

Oyama-san had arranged everything. Susan Osborn would sing, and her music would inspire me to paint. Seeing the painting in progress, she would then choose a song to go along with my work and influence it as she wished.

We spoke briefly before. It was to be a jam session. Susan's jazz background and her large repertoire were the perfect preparation. There was only an hour and a half of painting. Could I make it happen?

My mind was blank. Purposely so. Only so much preparation was possible. Before the performance, I felt a lot of tension behind stage, knowing I must be ready for any possible inspiration. I brought my largest brushes as well as my more delicate ones, and a variety of paints. Mami and I took hours to prepare them backstage.

We carefully taped black plastic sheeting to the stage floor and prepared the white nine-foot-square scroll on top of it for painting. Oyama-san arranged for the whole theater to be black to accentuate the large white square to be painted. Mami and I wore black.

We laid out all the paints and brushes, and Susan, in her red kimono, began to sing. Her rhythmic singing began like a soft breeze, and I painted the background as a feathery sky. Mami instinctively knew which brush to dip into which paint, before handing it to me. Susan watched as she sang. I could hear her sounds of acknowledgment between phrases. We were coordinating all our energy to drive the painting forward.

A tree trunk, branches—Mami replenished the brush with paint and had the next one ready when this one was spent. Now the leaves. It was a feverish chase against time to fill in enough leaves to make it rise to the level of the joyous sounds Susan was singing.

Between songs, I stepped back to survey my work. I would need the big brush for a large whirlpool of gold. Mami filled my six-foot brush with paint. It was my largest and heaviest brush. I drew my body up to wield the weight of it. It would take all my concentration, effort, and focus as my every motion would be dramatically preserved on a large scale.

Crouched and ready to spring, I asked for an encouraging shout. When Oyama-san shouted out from the front row, I sprang into action, letting fly the hairs of the brush. They flew above my head, separating in midair. When they slapped against the painting in progress, and the other drops fell in turn down the length of the scroll, I could hear the collective *Oh!* of the audience.

Slowly I pulled on the brush, bringing it toward me and around. The gold skeins of paint trailed, before and behind the leaves and branches I had just painted. The sight of this new addition was exciting but also challenging.

With this one act, I had disturbed the carefully created harmony of the painting beneath it. It was now up to me to make all elements of the painting harmonize while there was still time.

Susan began to sing, but hesitantly. She didn't want her song to determine my next important decision. How was I going to bring this whole painting together? Her quiet song helped me contemplate, but I mustn't spend too much time in thought.

Peonies? Yes. I started drawing large splashes of color for the beginnings of peonies. First, I needed the placement and volume right. The details could come later. Next, it was essential to watch the placement of my feet lest I smear the paint.

And then it happened. Susan began singing *Finlandia*, and it was sublime. Tears were in my eyes. I could feel Mami's hand quiver as she handed me the new brush. This was to be the ideal landscape of peace and harmony. The music opened before my eyes a vision of what I was to paint—as if I had only to trace what I was seeing before me. The petals, the leaves. The peonies came into focus.

Every moment was charged with tension and emotion until I suddenly found myself sobbing. There was no plan. No signal. But we both knew when it was done. Mami's cheeks were wet. I put my brush down as the music stopped. The lights were lowered, and I embraced her.

There was sniffling in the audience. While I had been painting, Mami had been dabbing at the places that were still wet. We took careful assessment of the painting and saw it was fine. I had attached a string to a pulley in the ceiling, and it was time to pull the painting up. The lights came up again. The painting could be seen hanging vertically for the first time.

I went to thank Susan, who gave me a big hug. Applause.

Mami's parents had been in the audience and were clearly moved. People came up to the stage to get a closer look, take photographs, and ask questions. It had been the most chilling, exciting, nerve-racking, and fulfilling collaboration of my life.

Oyama-san had planned the event to perfection. Susan had been completely in touch with each stage of my process. And years of Mami watching me in the studio had given her the intuition to know what I was going to need next.

The painting was about harmony.

So was the painting of it.

WE ALL HAVE A BAG

After my father died, I couldn't make myself cut my beard. The end of it reminds me that not that long ago, he saw it and approved. Stretched out, the brown tip reaches my navel. This is the part of my beard Dad saw. As time goes by, I feel it represents my father's role in my life.

Now it is mostly white, and three years of growth separate me from the end. Stretched out, it is more difficult to roll up and fasten with a pin under my chin. Hiding it this way makes it curly, and the kinks give it volume.

One day near the end of the year, I was on a crowded train. As it stopped with a lurch, I dropped the fastener from my beard. I couldn't find it without disturbing the person standing in front of me. As the crowd shuffled off, it disappeared under the chaos of feet. Beards can make people look aggressive, and I didn't want that.

A young mother and her boy of about three came in and looked up at me. The child seemed surprised. I didn't want to scare him. His mother sat down in the empty seat to my right, with shopping bags on her lap. Her son held the ones at her feet and stared at me.

I remembered that look. I have caused babies to bawl at the sight of me—a scary foreigner with prominent features. This boy looked at his mom, who then exchanged glances with me.

She asked, "Where are you from?" Despite their courtesy, the Japanese feel they have a right to this personal information from foreigners whom they will never see again. Often foreigners are assumed to be American, and people want to try out their English on me or get my perspective on the news.

I'm not always in the mood to discuss American politics, so on occasion, I have said I was from Germany or France. I learned my lesson one time when a fellow started speaking French to me; I had to feign arriving at my stop and leave the train prematurely.

Such a ploy felt wrong with this woman and her son, so I told her I could speak Japanese.

She was surprised and said, "You speak it very well."

Her son looked at her, then asked me, "Where do you live?"

I replied, "Would you like to guess?" If he thought I was Canadian, I was prepared to pretend he was correct.

"Yes," he said, "you're from the North Pole!"

I couldn't hide my surprise.

He took my reaction as confirmation and said, "I knew it!"

His mother explained, "He's been learning about Christmas at his preschool. And he's learning to say his numbers in English."

"Really? I'm impressed! Shall we say your numbers together?"

"Yeah."

"Yes," said his mother, correcting him.

"One ... two ... su ... sur ... three ...," and on to 10.

"Excellent!"

He grinned. "I've been really good!"

I glanced at his mother for confirmation and said, "I can see you have." The train stopped at Ikebukuro, and I stood.

"Don't go," he said.

"I'm so sorry," I explained. "You know how busy I am at this time of year. But I can see how good you are—just in the short time I've been with you."

"Shake?" He offered his hand.

Sandwiching his hand between both of mine, I hoped to communicate all the warmth I felt. His mother asked to shake my hand too.

When I had squeezed out through the closing door, I turned back to see people part before the window, making way for the two of them to wave at me. I gave them my cheeriest wave of the season until the train was out of the station.

There was a special alchemy to that event. That little boy helped me see my invisible Santa's bag.

I don't have a bag big enough to return to others what my father left me, or what Japan has taught me, or all the ways my life has been made for the better, but I enjoy the adventure that is life. I believe we all have reserves of strength, love, and sensitivity to draw on when needed. The more we share, the more of it appears in our bag.

I enjoy filling up my bag with reserves, finding the good in the world, improving my skills, doing my part. Sometimes surprises appear when I fumble around in my bag—usually a painting pops out.

WHAT A DIFFERENCE EIGHT YEARS MAKE

fter a number of years of cancellations and rescheduling, preparations for the Smithsonian exhibition had actually begun. The paintings for the Smithsonian's Renwick Gallery arrived safely in Washington, DC, and it was time to hang the show.

The walls were a deep gray. The platforms were ready and glowing gray as well. The wall text and captions had been silk-screened onto the wall, as I had done in my high school days. The assistants put on their white gloves and set up the paintings. The curator put on a surgical mask and went across each painting inch by inch, for insurance purposes.

This is no mere exaggeration. She scanned each panel of every painting with a magnifying glass, noting any irregularities on her clipboard and recording the location to the quarter inch.

"On the third panel, there is an embedded hair on forty-two by eight and what looks like a pistachio hull at sixty-five by four."

I raced over and looked where she indicated. There was indeed a pistachio hull trapped in the paint, almost invisible in the surrounding color. Last of all, the lighting was adjusted, and the paintings glowed.

I had addressed and sent out almost two hundred invitations to the opening party. I kept a few for any other people I may have forgotten.

While riding the subway from the Smithsonian to my parents' home, I remembered Grandby's Gallery and our bizarre encounter.

How long had it been? I could still see him swaying drunkenly in the doorway. I counted it out. It was almost exactly eight years since I heard him say, "Look, kid, if you're still painting, try again in eight years."

I got out just as the doors were opening on Dupont Circle. While ascending the subway's escalator, I pictured the expression on his florid face. Not only was I still painting, but I was exhibiting in a much better venue than his. I thought of how satisfying it would be to hand him the invitation to my solo exhibition at the Smithsonian, and my pace quickened. Even if he didn't see the irony in it, I suspected the woman would.

———————

I found the brownstone gallery, but it looked strange. It was abandoned. The sign had been taken down, and the unkempt building was dark and empty. I was not able to present my invitation because Grandby's prestigious gallery was no longer in business.

————

The night arrived for the opening party at the Smithsonian's Renwick Gallery. I had learned from previous gallery openings that guests must be able to tell at first glance that I am the artist. I wore something that served the purpose.

At the museum, the room was filled with people. Many had come from out of town. A golden light shining off my paintings illuminated people's faces during an exciting evening of reconnections and reunions. Time for the lecture arrived. I pulled out my carefully ordered box of slides. An assistant put them in the carousel, and I was ready.

Museum Director Elizabeth Broun came over to give me words of encouragement, and I gratefully remembered that day years ago when she had recommended I get better at speaking about my art.

On seeing my paintings projected, I immediately felt comfortable, and my words came easily. I had been asked to deliver lectures enough times by now that I knew the image of my paintings would turn the Grand Salon into my special space. I like to think of my art as a battery and that the energy I put into it as I paint can always be accessible to the viewer.

I explained the first slide. "This one with blue and green leaves is in a concert hall. The large maroon strokes you see were painted with a six-foot-long brush."

I clicked the advance button. "This is one I painted for a couple who moved to London. They wanted me to paint the things they were going to miss about their home in Tokyo."

I moved on to the next slide. "My experience with ceramics helped in making this twenty-foot ceramic mural that is in the lobby of the Japan Municipal Research Center." I could see the colors reflected in the glasses of the gentleman sitting in the front row. "I painted it to remind people of the historically renowned garden the building replaced."

I continued. "This next painting was inspired by the garden in Switzerland belonging to my friend Dante and his wife.

"Though I understand that this next one has since been stolen, it was originally commissioned for the executive suite of Takashimaya department store."

I went through the rest of the slides, and when the lecture was over, the floor was opened for questions. A hand shot up. A woman with cotton-candy hair pointed to the screen. "How much would you get for that one?" Heads turned, and she added, "That is, you know, roughly speaking …"

I didn't know how to answer. Museums aren't allowed to sell works. They aren't even allowed to introduce a buyer to me. I glanced at the curator.

"Well, uh … we can talk afterward."

As I was leaving, Elizabeth Broun said once again, "This isn't going to make your career. Nothing's going to change."

That was fine with me. This exhibition didn't need to define me. In the years since I first heard her say that, I had grown and become more confident. I had already changed so much.

This career was never going to be easy. It is the challenges that make the adventure fun. Being able to paint is what makes life sweet.

I came to Japan to improve *my* paintings—not to paint in the manner expected of nihonga artists. But after four decades here, I can no longer resist nor deny the influence Japan has had on me and my art. A woman at a recent exhibition told me that she liked how she thought my paintings made it possible for nihonga artists to paint in their own style and still be nihonga. I found freedom in my technique and a way of doing business that best suits my temperament. Perhaps that is how I fulfill Kayama sensei's expectations.

I was an outsider as an artist in America. And though I will never be Japanese, I'm surprised to find that as an artist here, I'm playing a meaningful role. I also found out that this barbarian no longer scares small children.

———

One recent autumn day, I was in my studio. I looked up at the sound of the door opening to see a very old man wearing a gray cardigan. He had a bald pate and a fidgety manner. He bowed stiffly and was hesitant to introduce himself, perhaps expecting me to recognize him. I did not.

"I have watched your career develop over the years," he said.

"Thank you. Feel free to step inside and look around if you're interested." He took off his shoes and stepped inside, approaching where I was working.

"Actually, I came to extend a, well, an invitation. I want you to feel welcome to use my pigment shop."

It was then I realized that this was the man who had refused to sell to me and locked me out of his store almost four decades before. He had sold only to the Five Mountains of Nihonga—recipients of honors from the emperor.

Deeply grateful, I thanked him. I was aware of the honor this invitation represented. Nevertheless, I realized I must respect the long relationships I had already developed with my other pigment shops.

FURTHER READING

Dear Reader—the following are just a few books
I return to often and strongly recommend:

Books on Japan

Zen Flesh, Zen Bones by Paul Reps
> This is a book of anecdotes that give a sense for how Japanese
> society operates in harmony and how to live the best possible life.

Stories from a Tearoom Window by Chikamatsu Shigenori
> We see how the values espoused by the great tea masters affect
> Japanese culture and aesthetic today.

Kokoro by Lafcadio Hearn
> Anecdotes of a foreigner show Japan in the 19th century as it began
> its dramatic shift toward Western-style modernization. See other
> books by this author.

Tokyo Station by Martin Cruz Smith
> This well-researched historical fiction by the author of *Gorky Park*

takes place in Tokyo immediately before and during the Second World War.

Lost Japan by Alex Kerr

This memoir provides a look at how contemporary Japan is changing and how traditional values are slipping away. Kerr's second book is *Dogs and Demons*, which takes this theme even further. I can recommend all his books on Japan.

Lonely Planet Guide to Japan by Rebecca Milner, Ray Bartlett, Andrew Bender, Stephanie d'Arc Taylor, Samantha Forge, Craig McLachlan, Kate Morgan, Thomas O'Malley, Simon Richmond, Phillip Tang, Benedict Walker

In the series, there are also editions focused on Tokyo, Kyoto, and so on. The curators have a good sense for the local life. Recommended for independent, adventurous travelers.

Books on Japanese Art

Masterpieces of Japanese Screen Painting: The American Collections by Miyeko Murase

Murase has authored so many excellent books on Japanese art that it's difficult to choose just one.

History of Art in Japan by Nobuo Tsuji

This is a broad survey of Japanese art. I can recommend his books on individual artists as well.

Ink and Gold: Art of the Kano by Felice Fisher

> The Kano school was the longest continual art movement in world history. It lasted over three hundred years. This excellent overview was created for the exhibition at the Philadelphia Museum of Art.

Rimpa: Decorative Japanese Painting by Toshinobu Yasumura

> This fat book is a feast of nothing but photographs of Rimpa school art. The publisher, PIE International, has a continuing series on Japanese art that includes almost no commentary.

Books on Western Art

The Faber Book of Art Anecdotes by Edward Lucie-Smith

> In this fascinating compilation, the foibles and intrigue of Western artists and the art world over the centuries are exposed.

Jackson Pollock: An American Saga by Steven Naifeh and Gregory W. Smith

> Naifeh and Smith bring to life a crucial time in the history of modern art. We see how critics abandoned Pollock in pursuit of the next art world darling.

Elaine and Bill, Portrait of a Marriage by Lee Hall

> Willem and Elaine de Kooning formed the partnership of two abstract expressionist painters.

Who Paid the Piper? by Frances Stonor Saunders

> This book describes the CIA's cultural propaganda program that changed the history of art in America—and to a degree, the world.

The Art of the Con by Anthony M. Amore

A peek into the underworld of contemporary art describes how the treatment of art as a financial instrument is corrupting culture.

BIBLIOGRAPHY

こんなに面白い東京国立博物館 April 21, 2005 新潮社.

Bowers, Faubion. *Japanese Theatre*. Rutland, VT: Charles E. Tuttle Company, 1974.

Gordon, Andrew. *A Modern History of Japan*. New York: Oxford University, 2003.

Hadfield, Peter. *Sixty Seconds That Will Change the World*. London: Pan MacMillan, 1992.

Henshilwood, C.S., J.C. Sealy, and R. Yates. "Blombos Cave, Southern Cape, South Africa: Preliminary Report on the 1992–1999 Excavations of the Middle Stone Age Levels." *Journal of Archaeological Science* 28, no. 4 (2001): 421–48.

Naifeh, Stephen, and Gregory W. Smith. *Jackson Pollock: An American Saga*. New York: Clarkson Potter, 1989.

Newman, John Henry. "The Pillar of the Cloud." *The British Magazine and Monthly Register*, 1834.

Reischauer, Edwin O. *The Japanese*. Cambridge: Belknap Press, 1978.

空知英秋, 銀魂, 第7巻（東京: 集英社, 2005）: 101-2.